Humanitarian Intervention

Crafting a Workable Doctrine

Three Options Presented as Memoranda to the President

Alton Frye, Project Director

A Council Policy Initiative

Sponsored by the Council on Foreign Relations

The Council on Foreign Relations, Inc., a nonprofit, nonpartisan national organization founded in 1921, is dedicated to promoting understanding of international affairs through the free and civil exchange of ideas. The Council's members are dedicated to the belief that America's peace and prosperity are firmly linked to that of the world. From this flows the mission of the Council: to foster America's understanding of other nations—their peoples, cultures, histories, hopes, quarrels, and ambitions—and thus to serve our nation through study and debate, private and public.

THE COUNCIL TAKES NO INSTITUTIONAL POSITION ON POLICY ISSUES AND HAS NO AFFILIATION WITH THE U.S. GOVERNMENT. ALL STATEMENTS OF FACT AND EXPRESSIONS OF OPINION CONTAINED IN ALL ITS PUBLICATIONS ARE THE SOLE RESPONSIBILITY OF THE AUTHOR OR AUTHORS.

This volume is the fourth in a series of Council Policy Initiatives (CPIs) designed to encourage debate among interested Americans on crucial foreign policy topics by presenting the issues and policy choices in terms easily understood by experts and nonexperts alike. The substance of the volume benefited from the comments of several analysts and many reviewers, but responsibility for the final text remains with the project director and the authors.

Other Council Policy Initiatives:

Future Visions for U.S. Defense Policy (1998; revised, 2000), John Hillen and Lawrence Korb, Project Directors; *Toward an International Criminal Court* (1999), Alton Frye, Project Director; *Future Visions for U.S. Trade Policy* (1998), Bruce Stokes, Project Director.

Council on Foreign Relations Books, Task Force Reports, and CPIs are distributed by Brookings Institution Press (1-800-275-1447). For further information about the Council or this paper, please write the Council on Foreign Relations, 58 East 68th Street, New York, NY 10021, or call the Director of Communications at 212-434-9400. Visit our website at www.cfr.org.

CONTENTS

FOREWORD

Humanitarian Intervention: Crafting a Workable Doctrine is the fourth in a series of Council Policy Initiatives (CPIs) launched by the Council on Foreign Relations in 1997. The purpose of a CPI is to illuminate diverse approaches to key international issues on which a policy consensus is not readily achievable. By clarifying a range of relevant perspectives on such issues, the Council hopes to inform and enhance the public debate over choices facing American foreign policy.

In pursuing that objective, a CPI follows a straightforward process:

1. Having chosen a topic of significance and controversy, the Council enlists knowledgeable authors of divergent opinions to argue the case for the policy option each would recommend to a U.S. president.

2. Each option takes the form of a memorandum that a senior government official might send to the president (or in some cases a draft speech that a president might deliver in presenting a decision to the American people).

3. Panels of other experts subject these drafts to critical review, an unofficial evaluation process that resembles interagency deliberations within the government.

4. After thorough revision, the papers are published under the cover of a memorandum arraying the options as a senior presidential adviser might do.

5. The published arguments then serve as the basis for debates in New York or Washington and meetings around the country.

The Council takes no institutional position on any policy question but seeks to present the best case for each plausible option a president—and fellow citizens—would wish to consider.

No challenge weighs more heavily on American foreign policy at the beginning of the 21st century than that of humanitarian intervention. The very concept is simultaneously an appeal to conscience and a caution to judgment. The relative immobilism of the Cold War has given way in many places to bloody chaos. Such chaos has emerged in more than one form and from more than one source—ethnic conflict, the collapse of states, the ruthlessness of factions competing for power. From Bosnia and Kosovo to Rwanda, East Timor, and Sierra Leone, the roster grows longer and the dilemmas grow deeper. Faced with massive violence against innocent human beings by their governments or by their neighbors, unrestrained or provoked by officials, what are other governments to do? Stand by? Or act forcefully, if necessary, to halt the killing and establish order?

The answer often hinges on whether the United States or other states are prepared to intervene with military force on the territory of another sovereign state. Whether it is possible to devise coherent, consistent guidelines for dealing with such crises is the focus of this CPI. The Council is greatly indebted to the study's principal authors, Arnold Kanter, Holly J. Burkhalter, Dov S. Zakheim, and Stanley A. McChrystal, for wrestling with perhaps the most perplexing problems the United States will face as it defines its role in a world afflicted with myriad humanitarian catastrophes. In conceiving and integrating the study, Alton Frye has enjoyed the able assistance of his colleague, Kathleen Houlihan.

As in so many Council endeavors, we owe special appreciation to Arthur Ross and his foundation. Their support has been indispensable in this CPI and in sustaining the Council's program to clarify major questions of foreign policy in ways that facilitate fruitful debate among interested Americans beyond the expert community.

Whoever occupies the Oval Office is likely to confront large-scale, man-made humanitarian disasters in other countries. Such episodes may well pose agonizing choices about whether to risk American lives and treasure to relieve them. Anticipating the need to make such choices and arraying the factors that bear upon them are surely the mandate of prudence. It is that mandate to which this CPI responds. The Council on Foreign Relations offers it as one contribution to the wider debate Americans must have in seeking common ground on this divisive subject.

Leslie H. Gelb
President, Council on Foreign Relations

ACKNOWLEDGMENTS

A Council Policy Initiative is a collective enterprise intended to nourish highly individual analyses. The authors have benefited from lively and astute exchanges with a distinguished panel of reviewers, whose tough-minded assessments strengthened even the arguments with which they disagreed. The Council is grateful to all who took part in the process of evaluating the manuscripts as they developed, including:

Project Director
and Editor: Alton Frye, *Council on Foreign Relations*

Panel
Reviewers: Ted G. Carpenter, *Cato Institute*
David A. Duffié, *Council on Foreign Relations*
Robert Filippone, *Office of Senator Bob Graham*
Arthur C. Helton, *Council on Foreign Relations*
Kenneth I. Juster, *Arnold & Porter*
Radha Kumar, *Council on Foreign Relations*
Charles Kupchan, *Council on Foreign Relations*
Robert A. Manning, *Council on Foreign Relations*
Kimber L. McKenzie, *Council on Foreign Relations*
William L. Nash, *National Democratic Institute for International Affairs*
Davis R. Robinson, *LeBoeuf, Lamb, Greene & MacRae*
Stephen S. Rosenfeld
Jon Rosenwasser, *Council on Foreign Relations*
Gordon C. Stewart, *Insurance Information Institute*

Research
  Associate and
  Rapporteur: Kathleen Houlihan, *Council on Foreign
                     Relations*

The memoranda are, of course, the work of the individual authors; no reviewer bears responsibility for any element of the CPI.

The writers owe a special debt to Patricia Dorff, the Council's director of publications, for shepherding the manuscript into finished form, and to Vice President and Publisher David Kellogg, for managing a production team of exemplary professionalism.

The project director and authors also wish to thank the Arthur Ross Foundation for enabling them to probe the essential, albeit confounding, contours of humanitarian intervention.

MEMORANDUM TO THE PRESIDENT

Arnold Kanter

FROM: "The National Security Adviser"

SUBJECT: Policy on "Armed Humanitarian Intervention"

During the more than forty years of the Cold War when we faced direct military threats to our national security and other vital interests, U.S. forces were employed with great rarity and even greater caution. Ironically, in the decade following the end of the Cold War and the collapse of the Soviet Union, we have threatened and used military force with increasing frequency in what has come to be called "armed humanitarian intervention." Had we yielded to all of the calls for help, we would have committed our military forces even more often.

Both you and your predecessors have been attacked from the Left and the Right over these past ten years, criticized by some for running needless risks and dissipating scarce resources by doing too much, and criticized by others for doing too little to stop moral outrages. It is hard to deny that despite our best efforts to articulate both a general policy on the use of U.S. military forces and specific rationales for particular decisions, the approach since the end of the Cold War has largely been ad hoc. One inevitable result has been not only the appearance but the reality of inconsistency. Why Kosovo and Haiti but not Rwanda or Sierra Leone? Why Bosnia but not Chechnya? Why Somalia but not Sudan?

The reasons for this inconsistency are readily understandable. On the one hand, we cannot and should not stand ready to intervene to right every wrong, and we will surely fail if we try. On the other hand, if we do not stand up for what we believe in and are not willing to make sacrifices to uphold our core values, we will both shirk our responsibilities and squander much of what has made our country special and great. Indeed, decisions about whether and when to intervene with military force in humanitarian crises are so hard in part because we cannot always say "yes" to whatever our consciences dictate, but we will not be able to live with ourselves if we never listen to those dictates. At the same time, there is no denying that this inconsistency has real costs both at home and abroad, starting with eroding domestic confidence and support, and with fostering a sense of unpredictability about U.S. responses that undermines the confidence of would-be coalition partners as well as the deterrent threat of intervention.

Not least because we are very likely to face more rather than fewer such problems in the future, we can and should do a better job of formulating and articulating a policy—or at least a set of guidelines—on when and where the United States will be prepared to commit its military forces to help mitigate or resolve man-made "humanitarian" crises. The goal is not to create rigid rules, but rather to strike a better balance between what should remain a pragmatic, case-by-case approach to difficult situations, and a reasonable pattern of consistency across those cases.

In the attached memoranda, your three senior national security advisers have proposed alternative approaches:

- The secretary of state believes that the United States has a vital interest in preventing and suppressing genocide and crimes against humanity, and in bringing their perpetrators to justice. She accordingly recommends a comprehensive initiative that includes a relatively expansive approach to the use of military force. Specifically, she proposes that when other means have failed, we be prepared to commit U.S. military forces in order to prevent, end, or preclude the resumption of "genocide" or "crimes against humanity" virtually anywhere these outrages are threatened or are being committed. She also recommends that specific military strategies and capabilities be developed to enhance the effectiveness of U.S. forces engaged in armed humanitarian interventions. The secretary underscores the pragmatic consideration that seeming American indifference to a pattern of man-made humanitarian crises will breed disorder and instability inimical to U.S. leadership in the 21ˢᵗ century.

- The secretary of defense recommends a much more restrictive approach to the use of military force. He argues that a relatively high threshold of facts and circumstances must be breached (for example, *clear* evidence of *genocide*) before intervention should be considered for purely humanitarian objectives. (In the interests of preserving alliance cohesion, the secretary of defense would be prepared to consider providing logistical support to allies who are directly engaged in armed humanitarian intervention.)

- As is appropriate for your senior military adviser, the chairman of the Joint Chiefs of Staff does not recommend a specific policy approach, but instead outlines a set of criteria and considerations for helping to decide whether, when, and how to intervene.

In essence, each of your three principal advisers proposes that you strike a different balance among the same set of competing considerations. In doing so, they elucidate a series of dilemmas that make decisions about committing U.S. military forces so difficult and agonizing. This covering memorandum highlights the key issues and choices you should consider in making your decisions about U.S. policy on armed humanitarian intervention. It also suggests some policy guidelines that can both help inform your decisions and increase the consistency among them.

WHAT IS "ARMED HUMANITARIAN INTERVENTION"?

The concept of "armed humanitarian intervention" and its various synonyms typically are vaguely defined and elusively broad. There is, however, a general consensus on at least some of its essential characteristics:

- It is "armed" in the sense that the threat and employment of military force is a central feature. That is, we clearly are not talking about sending personnel and equipment into nonhostile environments to provide relief from natural disasters such as a typhoon that strikes Bangladesh. We also mean something more than actions such as the water purification team and equipment dispatched to Rwanda in response to the man-made disaster there.

- It is "intervention" in the sense that it entails sending military forces across the sovereign borders or into the sovereign airspace of another country that has not committed international "aggression" against another state. Without getting bogged down in semantic disputes about whether armed humanitarian intervention entails the "offensive" or "defensive" employment of military force, we clearly are talking about something other than the well-understood concept of repelling or defeating an invasion across internationally recognized boundaries. On the contrary, armed humanitarian intervention constitutes an extreme case of interference in the internal affairs of another state.

- It is typically referred to as "humanitarian" because it entails the threat or use of U.S. force in situations that do not pose direct, immediate threats to U.S. strategic "interests." It is tempting to go on to say that it is "humanitarian" because it refers to circumstances in which our moral sense and human sensibilities are being massively assaulted. As will be discussed below, however, the term "humanitarian" should not be construed either narrowly or literally. First, even when our motives are relatively disinterested (at least in the sense that the defense of U.S. interests is not a principal reason for becoming involved), interventions inevitably have political consequences that make them anything but impartial in their effects. Indeed, efforts to behave as though we are impartial may be not only self-deceiving but also self-defeating in the sense that they inhibit action to deal decisively with the perpetrators of the outrage. Second, the very term "armed *humanitarian* intervention" borders on being an oxymoron in the sense that it entails the threat or use of violence for what purport to be humanitarian purposes. For reasons such as these, you should imagine quotation marks around the word "humanitarian" wherever it appears in this memo.

WHEN SHOULD WE INTERVENE?

While these parameters help to define what we mean by "armed humanitarian intervention," they both describe a much broader range of contingencies than we could ever imagine intervening in and fail to provide usable criteria for deciding where, when, and how to employ our military forces. We need somehow to narrow the scope of situations in which we would even consider intervention. In some ways, Rwanda is a litmus test. How we answer the question of whether Rwanda was a heart-wrenching but correct decision or a terrible mistake that we ought deeply to regret and vow never to repeat will say a lot about the purposes and premises of our policy.

Setting the Bar High

Your senior advisers generally attempt to circumscribe the problem by suggesting that consideration of the use of U.S. military forces be limited to those rare instances of "genocide," "crimes against humanity," or "war crimes." The secretary of defense, for example, recommends that you rely heavily on these categories, with particular emphasis on "genocide," as a way of sharply confining the circumstances in which the use of U.S. military force might be considered. Such an approach has the advantage of making clear that we will be highly selective and restrictive in our decisions about using military force in humanitarian interventions, confining ourselves to the most serious or egregious cases.

There is a real question, however, whether these three categories constitute either necessary or sufficient standards for determining when to intervene. Paradoxically, you may decide that these categories are too restrictive if we limit ourselves to the definitions of these terms as they are embodied in various international conventions, including the Rome Statute on the International Criminal Court (to which the United States is not a party). That is, they may both establish a presumption against intervention in situations in which our interests dictate otherwise, and create a strong expectation that we will intervene where we ultimately conclude we should not. For example, Kosovo arguably did not meet the test of "genocide" as defined in the international genocide convention, but Rwanda almost certainly did (and Chechnya might be close). One could argue that as a party to the Convention on the Prevention and Punishment of Genocide, we would have been obliged to intervene in Rwanda (and perhaps Chechnya) to stop the genocide, but that same agreement offers neither obligation nor rationale for our intervention in Kosovo.

In fact, unless we are prepared to adopt a broader (or at least more complex and nuanced) standard, such as intervening to prevent or stop gross human rights abuses or other serious oppression, we would be hard put to develop a consistent rationale to explain most of the armed humanitarian interventions in which the United States participated during the 1990s. But unless it were otherwise qualified or limited, such a broader standard would make it that much more difficult both to be selective in determining whether and when to intervene with military force, and to avoid a continuing pattern of ad hoc, inconsistent policy. In this connection, one need only consider whether and how we implement what appeared from official U.S. statements to be an unqualified public commitment to intervene again in any "future Kosovos."

Pursuing an "Interest-Based" Policy
In the search for criteria that would define a policy that is, at once, consistent and selective, one is tempted to say that we should be prepared to intervene with military force only in those situations in which key U.S. interests are importantly engaged. Applying such a standard, however, gives one less purchase on the issue than might be imagined. First, a policy of refusing to deploy military force except in those cases in which "vital" U.S. national interests are threatened would be so highly restrictive as to be tantamount to an intervention policy that treated any and all "humanitarian" considerations as superfluous, and of refusing to participate in virtually any and every case of *humanitarian* intervention.

Second, the debate about pursuing either an "interest-based" foreign policy or a more Wilsonian (or "idealist") foreign policy often is not productive because it turns on a distinction between "interests" and "values" that, in practice, amounts to a false dichotomy. Not only is it very much in the U.S. national interest to foster an international environment that is compatible with our values—including democratic norms, human rights, and free markets—but from a purely pragmatic perspective, our moral authority is an indispensable element of American leadership and influence. Moreover, we as Americans sooner or later must face ourselves, live with the consequences of our action or inaction, and decide what it says about who we are and what we stand for. All of your senior advisers share this perspective, at least to the extent that they believe the United States should be prepared to consider the use of military force in clear cases of genocide.

Third and related, a rigid insistence that key U.S. interests be at stake before we will consider armed humanitarian intervention can create irresistible pressures to concoct "interest-based" rationalizations for interventions that are undertaken for essentially humanitarian or other "value" reasons. Bosnia and, to a lesser extent, Kosovo, are cases in point. Not only do such efforts at rationalization elicit skepticism or worse, but they also cloud hard-nosed assessments of U.S. interests and compel rhetorical contortions that come back to haunt us.

In the end, the U.S. interests at stake—which ones and how much—in a particular "humanitarian" contingency are better treated not as a threshold standard, but rather as one—but only one—of the key factors you will need to weigh in making decisions about the use of military force.

Preventive Measures

The secretary of state proposes a quite different approach to limiting the employment of U.S. military force. She recommends that your policy place great emphasis on "preventive" measures that, if successful, could limit, if not preclude, the need to use force, as well as reduce the severity and duration of the humanitarian crisis. The secretary of defense likewise looks to "preventive measures" as a way to minimize the commitment of U.S. forces.

There is no denying that, if we are going to intervene, it usually is better to do so sooner rather than later when the humanitarian tragedy has gotten worse, and when the costs and risks of intervention have gotten higher. That said, you and your predecessors have found it very difficult to translate this principle into practice.

From a policy perspective, you will face an inherent dilemma. On the one hand, treating armed humanitarian intervention as an extraordinary rather than a routine event requires that the bar to military intervention be set high. That, in turn, often means waiting until there is clear evidence of widespread atrocities. On the other hand, preventive measures usually require intervening before the situation has irretrievably deteriorated. That, in turn, may require you to act before reliable information is available, and before it is clear where and how far the situation is headed. The speed with which a humanitarian crisis can develop and potential genocide can spread increases the premium on taking actions that may, in retrospect, prove to have been unwarranted or excessive.

A policy of "preventive interventions" likewise is unlikely to help you much with your political problems. First, it will be hard to muster the domestic political support you will need to take preemptive actions, if only because the present costs of acting almost always seem much clearer and greater than the future risks of not acting. For related reasons, it also may prove difficult to muster much participation from others, which, in turn, will make it that much more difficult to create and sustain the domestic consensus you will need. (A doctrine of "preventive intervention" also could be readily exploited by some states as a virtual blank check to interfere in other countries' internal affairs.)

Second, as will be noted below, once the United States becomes involved, and especially once U.S. military forces become involved, the costs and consequences of failing to achieve our stated objectives can increase dramatically. This means that if seemingly low-cost preventive interventions are not successful, you will have to choose between incurring the costs of escalating our military intervention and paying the near-term and long-term prices to U.S. interests of starting something we are not prepared to finish. Worse, the political imperatives to impose sharp limits on "preventive" interventions are at odds with a prudent military strategy of acting decisively, and increase the chances that you will face such an unpalatable choice. If you have not secured congressional support for the initial preventive intervention and the risks that it entails, it is a virtual certainty that you will be subjected to intense political attacks no matter which course you choose.

Third, while preventive interventions may initially be less costly, there is no assurance that—if "successful"—they can avoid many of the costs and risks noted below that often attend larger-scale armed humanitarian interventions.

Put simply, the number of "potential" humanitarian crises we will face is likely to be much larger than the number of crises in which we can—or should—consider even limited forms of "preventive" military intervention. Such preventive interventions may be important policy instruments once you decide to act, but a declaratory policy of preventive intervention is unlikely to limit the occasions when you will be confronted with decisions about the prospective use of U.S. military force, or to provide a way to help you make those decisions.

Division of Labor

You and your predecessors sometimes have tried to employ a kind of "division of labor" approach in an effort to limit U.S. participation in armed humanitarian interventions. Under various formulations, this has amounted to a policy of leaving such interventions to others unless the United States possessed unique military capabilities that were required, and then limiting our role in these cases to those functions (for example, lift, intelligence, communications) in which U.S. forces have a comparative advantage. A variant of this approach is to limit U.S. involvement to levels that are commensurate with the magnitude of the atrocity; for example, even serious human rights abuses might warrant no more than modest U.S. involvement, while we might be prepared to intervene with more substantial military force in cases of genocide. The early debates about, and then initial U.S. engagement in, Bosnia provide a good illustration of this approach.

A policy along these lines has obvious attractions. First, and most apparent, it would help to circumscribe U.S. military intervention. In doing so, it would help to reduce the risks to our people, the erosion of our capabilities, and the raid on our treasury. Second, it has an appealing and easy-to-understand logic. Third, it should make it more difficult for others—when they have both the responsibility and the wherewithal to fill the role—to yield to the temptation of leaving the difficult and dirty work of armed humanitarian interventions to us.

As we have learned from experience, however, such an approach also has drawbacks. If we do not take the initiative—even in those cases in which the United States has no specific responsibility or historical connection—we have often found that, far from prodding others into action, it provides a convenient excuse for them to do nothing. We also should recognize that the United States not only has unique military capabilities but also possesses unmatched political capacity to mobilize others. If we refuse to act except in those cases in which only we have the required forces, we must then be prepared to see everyone joining us on the sidelines while the atrocities proceed, and to pay the price in terms of damage to our assertions of moral leadership (and to our consciences).

At the same time, it is difficult to exercise leadership if we appear to be—much less are—unwilling to share the resulting risks and costs. We therefore need to be candid in acknowledging that by limiting ourselves to participating in roles in which we have a comparative military advantage, we typically are reserving to ourselves precisely those roles that carry the least risk. At a minimum, such a division of labor undermines any claims we might assert that the United States must have the lead in decisions about strategies and tactics. It also risks fueling resentment about the nature and limits of U.S. participation that could well spill over onto other issues and relationships, if not cynicism regarding U.S. claims about its concerns and commitments.

A related consideration concerns the implications of the commitment of U.S. military power. As a rule, we want any potential adversary to believe that once U.S. forces are committed, we are likewise committed to achieving our objectives and that our adversary cannot expect to wear us down, much less drive us out, by raising the ante. If we insist on limiting our participation to certain military roles and then things go badly on the ground, we will face a choice between expanding our role and putting that principle in jeopardy.

These considerations combine to place what may be an inordinate share of the burden on American shoulders for determining whether and how to respond to humanitarian crises, but they cannot be ignored. At the same time, they do not oblige us to solve all the world's problems by ourselves. There is a vast difference between leadership and unilateral action. Indeed, the challenge of exercising leadership is to ensure that others follow and do their fair share.

FEASIBILITY AND EFFECTIVENESS OF
ARMED HUMANITARIAN INTERVENTIONS

As the world's sole remaining superpower, we almost reflexively assume that we have the military wherewithal to resolve, if not prevent, virtually any man-made humanitarian crisis. That assumption, however, needs to be critically assessed every time we are faced with such a decision because recent history suggests that, even if considerations of costs and risks are ignored, it may not be valid. As noted above, we likewise need to be clear-eyed about the paradox of employing distinctly nonhumanitarian means (that is, the application of military power that is designed to kill people and break things) in an effort to achieve humanitarian ends.

Indeed, if one were to generalize from the cases of Somalia, Haiti, Bosnia, and Kosovo, one might conclude that the threatened or actual employment of U.S. force may be relatively effective in fostering and enforcing a cessation of widespread violence but can make little or no contribution to mitigating the conditions that led to the atrocities, to building or rebuilding the necessary political and other institutions, or to nurturing reconciliation and the norms of a civil society. Those same cases also suggest that the economic, political, and other nonmilitary means we have at our disposal either have not been employed effectively or have not proven very potent in addressing these issues.

Stopping the killing and preventing further atrocities are no small accomplishments, but the record to date suggests that even our "successful" interventions have been less a matter of buying time than of stopping the clock. Put differently, these experiences suggest that we can be relatively successful in controlling a situation so long as we maintain our military presence, but they also suggest that little else will have changed and that the situation could readily revert to that which prevailed prior to our intervention soon after we depart.

This cold reality, in turn, may regularly confront us with the choice among three unattractive options: (a) maintaining military forces indefinitely in these trouble spots, (b) being willing to accept a return to those conditions and outrages that prompted our intervention in the first place, and confronting difficult questions about what our sacrifices have accomplished, or (c) dropping all pretense of impartiality, choosing sides between the protagonists, and going to war to defeat the newly designated "enemy." Whatever the choice, it likely will serve to increase the political obstacles to future humanitarian interventions, even when other factors might incline us to become involved. It also may cast the concept, to say nothing of the content, of "exit strategies" in a whole new light.

As we consider armed humanitarian interventions, we accordingly need to be very hard-nosed about what can—and cannot—be accomplished by the deployment of military force, rather than just yield to an overwhelming sense of frustration and an irresistible urge to "do something" when other means to deal with moral outrages have been found wanting. This means being explicit and precise about at least the following:

1. What the overall political objective is.

2. What the military mission is.

3. What the military mission is expected to accomplish.

4. How—and how much—accomplishing that mission will help achieve the political objective.

5. What the plan is (and what that plan's prospects are) for filling whatever gap remains between accomplishing the military mission and achieving the political objective.

Performing this kind of analysis may well reveal that we are about to grab hold of another tar baby. Such a conclusion does not necessarily lead to the conclusion that we should not intervene but should at least help illuminate what we are getting ourselves into.

COSTS AND CONSEQUENCES OF ARMED HUMANITARIAN INTERVENTIONS

Even if we determine that an armed humanitarian intervention is likely to succeed, we still need to gauge whether such a success is worth the costs, risks, and consequences the action could entail.

Most obvious, not only can military interventions cost considerable sums over and above the annually appropriated defense budget for which the money must be found, but they also can exact real and substantial costs to U.S. military capabilities in training foregone, wear and tear on equipment, and strains on morale and personnel retention. In combination, this means that the more we participate in armed humanitarian interventions, the less capable our forces will be in carrying out what most Americans believe are their primary missions and responsibilities, and the more other defense and domestic priorities will be shortchanged. More fundamentally, if through either policy or circumstance we expect to become more rather than less involved in armed humanitarian interventions in the future, we need to face the question of whether we should reconfigure at least some of our forces so that they are better suited to carry out what turn out to be relatively distinctive missions.

There are other dangers for the United States as well. By their very nature, armed humanitarian interventions pose real risks that American service personnel will be killed or injured. As the secretary of defense observes, we not only should satisfy ourselves that the humanitarian crisis at hand warrants the distinctly nonhumanitarian act of killing but that it is a cause worth dying for. (We must also acknowledge that reducing the risks to our military personnel often increases the risks—perhaps substantially—to innocent people on the ground.) As evidence mounts of the reach of international terrorism, we should be mindful that Americans at home could become innocent victims of U.S. participation in armed humanitarian interventions abroad, the so-called blow-back phenomenon.

Assessing the potential consequences—including the unintended consequences—of our intervention for the situation on the ground is a prerequisite. As we learned in Somalia, it could prove to be difficult, if not impossible, to remain even-handed and above the fray. On the contrary, the longer we stay and the more we try—or have to try—to accomplish, the more likely it is that we will find ourselves becoming entangled and taking sides.

Likewise there is no assurance that our intervention will make things better—except perhaps temporarily—and it could make things worse. For example, it is at least arguable that the initiation of air attacks on Kosovo by the North Atlantic Treaty Organization (NATO) accelerated, if not intensified, the depredations the Serbs visited on the Kosovar Albanians. It also must be asked whether we created or contributed to a moral hazard—that is, did the prospect of NATO intervention encourage the Kosovo Liberation Army (KLA) provocations aimed at eliciting Serb retributions, which, in turn, made NATO intervention more likely? (Such moral hazards also can proliferate if dissident groups elsewhere conclude that stepping up the violence will prompt U.S. intervention to their advantage.) Finally, one must wonder about the extent to which ethnic cleansing by the Serbs has been replaced by ethnic cleansing by the Kosovar Albanians, and how much responsibility we must accept for that outcome.

Broader and less tangible issues also are at stake. By their nature, armed humanitarian interventions almost always entail violating the sovereignty of a state and interfering in its internal affairs. If not entirely in the eyes of the beholder, it must at least be granted that there often is a fine line between an "invasion" and an "armed humanitarian intervention." (The line may be even finer between "preventive intervention" and "interference in internal affairs.") This may be less of a concern and problem in the case of "failed states" such as Somalia, where, it could be argued, there was no government that could perform the basic functions of preserving internal order, much less had standing to approve or object to an intervention force. We do, however, face the issue squarely in the case of "oppressive states" such as Serbia, whose sovereignty over Kosovo we have repeatedly reaffirmed. (Ironically, it probably is more pertinent, if not necessarily easier, to use the threat or fact of armed intervention to try to deter or coerce an "oppressive state" that can exercise effective control over its population and military forces than a "failed state" that cannot.)

By itself, the principle of national sovereignty may not be an absolute bar to armed humanitarian interventions, but it should constitute a substantial presumption against intervening that must be surmounted by the compelling nature of the particular circumstances. In addition to the obvious international legal considerations, the concept of state sovereignty has powerful pragmatic benefits that should not be ignored, particularly in the absence of an equally powerful principle for organizing and managing the international system that could take its place. One need only consider the alternative—that is, a world in which governments are free to interfere in one another's internal affairs, and an international free-for-all as various countries and coalitions assert a unilateral "right" of humanitarian intervention, including in ways that are directly counter to key U.S. interests. Put simply, one should think long and hard before declaring that the Treaty of Westphalia is obsolete.

One way to try to square this sovereignty circle is to obtain a U.N. imprimatur on any armed humanitarian intervention. Although a different kind of military action for a different purpose, the Gulf War illustrates the utility of securing authorization from the U.N. Security Council. At the same time, we have learned that we must have alternatives to U.N. approval for legitimizing actions we believe are required, not least because—as Kosovo and other recent cases illustrate—we cannot always be assured of getting the kind of Security Council resolution we believe is needed.

As Kosovo also demonstrates, however, not all international imprimaturs are equal. Circumventing the United Nations and relying on the North Atlantic Treaty to legitimize our intervention may have been preferable, and perhaps even unavoidable, but it has had real immediate and longer-term costs. Not only did it send an unmistakable message to Moscow and Beijing about our (un)willingness to take their concerns into account, thus making the Security Council less useful and pliable the next time we seek its authorization for interventions we believe are necessary; it also invites others to turn to—or invent—alternative international institutions to sanction actions that are contrary to U.S. interests.

ILLUSTRATIVE POLICY GUIDELINES

As this recitation of concerns, considerations, and dilemmas makes clear, it is naïve to expect that we can formulate a set of "iron laws" that constitute the policy we will follow on armed humanitarian interventions in each and every case. Moreover, defining such a policy would be unwise because doing so would hamstring you and your successors on an issue on which you desperately need to preserve flexibility. It should be possible, however, to articulate some principles and guidelines that help to frame policy responses that will be relatively predictable and consistent over a number of cases.

What follows are some potential candidates you may want to bear in mind as you review the attached memos from your three senior advisers. As you will see, these guidelines combine to establish a strong presumption against armed humanitarian intervention. At the same time, however, they seek to avoid the need to make first-order judgments either about what U.S. interests must be at stake, or an "atrocity threshold" that needs to be exceeded, before U.S. participation in an armed humanitarian intervention will even be considered.

1. *Determine that this is a crisis that matters significantly to the United States.* As noted above, this determination is likely to be some combination of important interests and values that are at stake. Taken together, however, they need to be clearly worth the always-substantial costs and risks that will be entailed. It also should be noted that this is a decision for you to make rather than one that is forced upon you: while modern media have become an important political force, humanitarian crises ranging from Rwanda to Chechnya demonstrate that the "CNN effect" need not compel you to act contrary to your determination of U.S. interests and values at stake.

2. *Determine that U.S. participation will make the critical political or military difference.* We should neither reflexively fill the void left by the inaction of others nor stand inflexibly aloof from a crisis that matters to us, but does not demand our unique military capabilities. We should instead proceed pragmatically, determining in each case whether the form and magnitude of our participation is warranted both by the stakes involved and the willingness of others to respond to our leadership.

3. *Determine that sufficient domestic political support not only can be created but also can be sustained even in the face of unpleasant developments and unexpected costs.* The so-called zero casualty doctrine is not an essential feature of armed humanitarian interventions but rather is an artifact of the unwillingness or failure of political leaders to make the case for intervention to the American people. The American people will pay the price—both human and monetary—of U.S. intervention if they are convinced it is worth it. If serious efforts to persuade them and their elected representatives fail, then that should be a strong argument against intervening. As a corollary, we should not even

consider armed humanitarian interventions in cases in which we would have to face a substantial military opponent. The humanitarian impulse cannot justify committing the United States to a major war. One need look no further than Chechnya.

4. *Resist any temptation to go it alone.* For both domestic and international political reasons, meaningful participation by other states should be a central feature of any armed humanitarian intervention in which the United States is involved. Likewise, international sanction for the operation, preferably from the U.N. Security Council, should be obtained. Unilateral armed humanitarian interventions by the United States should be all but ruled out.

5. *Clearly define the political objective.* Assessments of the role, relevance, and risks of employing military power cannot be made without a clear and precise specification of the overall goal to be achieved. It is one thing to intervene to stop mass violence, but quite another to use force to defeat one of the protagonists (that is, the "oppressor" or "perpetrator"), and still another to create the institutions and environment on which a secure and just civil society rests.

6. *Clearly define and carefully circumscribe the military mission.* Doing so may be unsatisfying as well as politically unpopular, but there may be no other way to have a reasonable prospect both of accomplishing the mission and of avoiding becoming a partisan on one side or the other. The transition in mission from humanitarian relief to disarming the protagonists in Somalia is a case in point. At the same time, we should not limit—at least not publicly—the military means we are prepared to use to accomplish that mission (for example, announce at the outset that the U.S. role will be confined to air strikes).

7. *Have very high confidence of success.* Do not consider armed humanitarian intervention unless (a) there is a clear military mission, (b) there is a very high probability that the military mission will be achieved, and (c) accomplishment of that mission is tantamount to achieving the desired political objective, or there

is high confidence that the additional non-military means required to achieve the objective will be employed and will be successful.

8. *Make clear that we mean what we say, and that we will finish what we start.* Demonstrating this determination will be important not only for its immediate effect on the crisis at hand, but also for its effect on future would-be oppressors. In the post–Cold War world no less than during the Cold War, credibility remains the essence of deterrence and coercion. The alternative (as our inaction in Rwanda may indicate) is that both we and potential perpetrators learn the no-more-Somalias/never-again lesson. Observing this principle, however, will require that a decision to commit *any* U.S. forces is tantamount to a decision to commit whatever U.S. force proves to be needed to succeed. (Indeed, once the United States intervenes with military force, the reasons that led to the intervention may become an almost secondary consideration in determining how to proceed. On that point the "quagmire" that Vietnam became, although very different in nature, is the object lesson.) It also will require careful discipline to ensure that our rhetoric does not outrun our capabilities or political will. Otherwise, deterrence will be diminished and the risks of miscalculation will increase.

The memoranda that follow demonstrate both the necessity and the difficulty of applying systematic judgment to those humanitarian contingencies that raise the question of armed intervention.

MEMORANDUM TO THE PRESIDENT

Holly J. Burkhalter

FROM: "The Secretary of State"

SUBJECT: Intervention to Stop Mass Killing or Genocide

One of the most urgent foreign policy questions this administration must address is determining what role the United States will play when governments or insurgent forces commit massive abuses against unarmed people. These issues are too important to descend to caricature, contrasting an expansive but distorted view of a "Clinton Doctrine" with an oversimplified and unrealistic alternative that would spare us hard choices by ruling out the hard cases.

The U.S. government has been denounced by some for doing too much in response to human rights crises (with Kosovo and Haiti receiving particular criticism) and by others for doing too little, especially with regard to the Rwanda genocide. Mass killings of civilians are certain to occur somewhere in the world during your presidency, and it is essential that this administration have in place a policy and a program for addressing the issue. The most difficult and controversial feature of such a policy will be the use of military force to prevent or stop crimes against humanity, and particularly the question of deploying American soldiers.

MASS KILLINGS THREATEN U.S. INTERESTS

The central premise of a new U.S. policy on humanitarian military intervention should be that mass killings of unarmed men, women, and children are a threat to American vital interests. Preventing and stopping them should be among this nation's top foreign policy commitments. Many people make the case that this government should contemplate intervention only to stop mass killings when such crimes endanger U.S. material, geopolitical, or commercial interests. In my view, unchecked mass killing anywhere is a threat to global peace and stability, and thus to American interests. Each such occasion requires an active and concerted diplomatic and political effort commensurate with the resources and international stature of the United States. On some occasions, effective action to suppress genocide or crimes against humanity may require an American military response as well.

Warring parties or abusive governments that inflict atrocities upon the innocent as a means of broadening or retaining their power challenge the conscience of the world. It is morally imperative that the American president proclaim and act upon the conviction that such crimes will not be tolerated. The inherent integrity of individual human beings is a universal value embodied in the founding of this country, in our Constitution, and in the international human rights treaties we have signed. Unrestrained depredations against innocent men, women, and children are an assault on these values and upon human dignity everywhere.

This moral imperative should not be seen as separate from, competitive with, or antithetical to other American interests. The moral necessity of countering crimes against humanity is inextricably linked to pragmatic and self-interested reasons for action. Just as it is in America's vital national interest to deter those who engage in international terrorism, drug trafficking, nuclear proliferation, and environmental degradation, so too is it in our vital interest to prevent and quell mass killings of noncombatants, wherever such crimes occur.

The challenge to American policy is to understand the ways in which humanitarian crises seemingly distant from our national interests, as conventionally defined, can generate major problems in areas more central to those interests. A world of creeping disorder is hardly congenial to U.S. interests, and the notion that "local" humanitarian crises can be left to burn themselves out with no serious impact on the United States is dubiously optimistic. If the Cold War domino theory deserves the ill repute into which it has fallen, one should be equally wary of the blithe assumption that indifference to human rights abuses in one setting will have little consequence in others. Avoiding a pattern of powerlessness—or worse, indifference—by leading nations in the face of man-made humanitarian catastrophes is a matter of palpable importance to the United States.

Genocide does not affect the immediate economic and physical well-being of Americans at home, but it degrades the world we live in as does nothing else. Mass killings dangerously destabilize the countries where they occur by fomenting and spreading armed conflict, destroying institutions of civil society, and eliminating large sections of the population, frequently including the country's intellectual, political, and economic elite. Such abuses can wipe out years of development and contribute to the collapse of the state altogether.

The danger is by no means limited to the country where killings are committed. The world's tolerance of atrocities and their perpetrators encourages others who might be tempted to target vulnerable minorities or exterminate major sectors of the population as a means of gaining or retaining power. Mass murder of civilians destabilizes entire regions, creating flows of refugees that materially burden and politically undermine neighboring countries. The deliberate exacerbation of ethnic tensions by practitioners of genocide or other massive violations often spills across borders, spreading violence and physical destruction.

Preventing and stopping crimes against humanity implicates American interests as well because of the terrible toll that they take on international institutions. The prestige and effectiveness of the United Nations and its strongest member states were damaged severely by failure to forestall the Rwanda genocide and by years of atrocities that took place in Bosnia under the very eyes of a sizable peacekeeping contingent.

Unchecked atrocities can put U.N. personnel themselves at risk. U.N. blue helmets are not combat troops. They are in a poor position to defend civilian populations and to stabilize fragile post-conflict situations if other measures have not first been taken to stop the atrocities. It is in the U.S. national interest that the United Nations carry out peacekeeping successfully. Placing the institution in situations like that of Sierra Leone in May 2000, where 500 U.N. peacekeepers were taken hostage by the Revolutionary United Front (RUF) insurgency, endangers the organization and its personnel and weakens its ability to carry out its duties elsewhere.

Finally, if the United States expects to retain its political leadership in the world, it must not be derelict when the slaughter of innocents occurs. The world looks to the United States for leadership when such depredations threaten. In cases such as Bosnia and Kosovo, the governments of Europe, which had the most immediate stake in stopping crimes against humanity, nonetheless refused to act without the political and military involvement of the United States. The United States, which leads in almost every other international endeavor, cannot simply exempt itself when mass murder of unarmed people unfolds.

Widespread atrocities against civilians cannot be kept secret. The explosion of communications technology means that genocide halfway across the globe reaches the eyes of the American public in real time. When Americans are confronted with tragedies, they expect and demand a response from their government. This so-called CNN effect is neither cynical nor superficial. It is a clear indication that the American people are less isolationist and more sympathetic to humanitarian activism than are many of their elected representatives in Congress.

At the same time, the American people will not tolerate the squandering of American soldiers' lives in ill-considered, inappropriate, or counterproductive interventions. Raising the prevention and suppression of mass killings to the level of a U.S. vital interest does not mean that the United States must respond with military force every time unarmed people are killed in large numbers. Those occasions that require American military engagement will likely be very few indeed, particularly if you undertake a vigorous political and diplomatic campaign to prevent or respond to crimes in their early stages.

Regrettably, however, even the most energetic program to prevent such slaughters will not always succeed, and you will inevitably face circumstances where nothing appears to deter those bent on large-scale butchery. Every instance where civilians are massacred in large numbers with the initiative or acquiescence of governmental authorities or organized insurgencies requires some response, but not every such occasion necessitates an American military response. It is morally defensible to limit sharply those occasions on which U.S. military force is contemplated, but only if the criteria used to make that determination are informed by human rights considerations. Because warding off or halting genocide and like crimes is a moral cause, the choices that you make in response must be morally comprehensible as well.

I propose a criterion for evaluating the potential deployment of American soldiers that is rigorously pragmatic with respect to human rights objectives and outcomes. Because warfare generally has profoundly negative consequences for civilians, the decision to use American force must take into account the implications of military intervention on the lives of unarmed men, women, and children—both those at risk of extermination and those potentially at risk from international intervention itself. These considerations will limit those occasions in which the United States deploys its own forces to stop crimes against humanity, but it is a very different criterion than that customarily proposed by the opponents of humanitarian intervention. Conventional criteria invariably rule out intervention if U.S. commercial, material, or strategic interests are not implicated. In the rationale proposed here, limitations on the use of American military force are imposed by humanitarian considerations themselves.

The following questions should be answered when considering whether the United States should deploy its troops to counter genocide or crimes against humanity:

I. General Criteria

1. Are killings of civilians part of an organized campaign by insurgent or government forces who have purposely targeted large numbers of civilians or who threaten to do so?

2. Have measures short of warfare to deter perpetrators and defend their victims been tried in good faith and exhausted?

3. What is the least invasive form of military intervention that can be employed that will be effective in stopping abuses and saving the largest number of lives?

4. Does the intervention preserve or revert to a status quo that is grossly abusive? Are perpetrators left in positions of authority? Will civilians remain at risk or be placed at heightened risk from them or others once international forces depart?

5. Do the life-saving benefits of the contemplated military action outweigh the potential cost in human lives, particularly if the perpetrators possess significant military capability, such as access to weapons of mass destruction? Do the military tactics under consideration themselves cause significant or disproportionate civilian casualties?

II. Criteria Specific to the United States

6. Are certain features of American military prowess uniquely required for the best possible human rights outcome? If others are available to intervene effectively and can do so with minimum harm to civilians and material damage to the country in question, can the United States aid those efforts without sending its own forces?

7. Could aspects of U.S. military doctrine (such as the use of overwhelming force, and the zero-casualty norm) contribute to human rights problems in and of themselves?

8. If the United States refuses to send military forces, does that decision militarily and politically complicate or foreclose the option for others?

9. Does military intervention by the United States have the potential of widening the conflict by drawing in other parties, in ways that military intervention by others would not?

10. What are the costs in human lives of the United States's refusing to engage militarily? What actions might our government take to compensate?

The purpose of this practical framework for considering military intervention is not to rule out American military intervention, but rather to assure that American forces, when they are deployed, are employed in ways that offer the best hope for quelling mass killings and preventing their recurrence. As these criteria indicate, there will be occasions where human rights considerations themselves preclude the deployment of American troops, even when genocide threatens. Especially in those cases, the United States will bear a heavy obligation to find other ways to help end the killing and subdue the perpetrators. This memorandum includes a number of recommendations in this regard.

The foregoing set of questions suggests some of the human rights problems that are raised when American military force is contemplated. Part of our task in developing a forceful and effective policy in this field will be to address these human rights contradictions. Deploying U.N. forces for peacekeeping, monitoring, or policing has become commonplace in recent years, but occasions where military force is deployed in nonconsensual situations to stop violations and protect civilians are very rare. Indeed, neither the United Nations nor its strongest members have developed a military doctrine for such a use of force, and there are virtually no precedents for military operations expressly designed to save civilians when massacres by well-armed and organized forces are at their height.

Some of the international community's greatest failings in the face of organized violence against unarmed people stem from this vacuum in military strategy and experience. On the one hand, the United Nations has attempted to protect civilians without engaging militarily to stop, defeat, or demobilize those who prey upon them. The peacekeeping experience in Bosnia is replete with horrifying examples of the consequences of such an approach: the creation of protected corridors that were routinely assaulted by the Bosnian Serb army, the establishment of safe havens that became death camps when overrun by those same forces, the deployment of international monitors who could watch but not protect victims, and the introduction of U.N. peacekeepers who themselves became hostages of hostile soldiers.

The U.S. and allied experience in Kosovo represents the other end of the spectrum. There, NATO undertook actions appropriately aimed at securing the withdrawal of Serb forces from the province, but the military operations did nothing actually to protect civilians in the meantime. The result was a campaign of high-altitude bombing that eventually secured the withdrawal of the Yugoslav army and special forces from the province but failed to stop the killing and expulsion of massive numbers of ethnic Albanians, which actually accelerated dramatically while the bombing took place.

In my view, when killings of civilians have reached such proportions that international military action is contemplated, that action should be directed toward defeating, expelling, or demobilizing the perpetrators of those crimes and the apprehension of those who commanded them to face independent investigation and prosecution. At the same time, such operations must not ignore noncombatants at immediate risk, much less heighten their vulnerability.

PREVENTING AND RESPONDING TO
ORGANIZED MASS MURDER

The great human tragedies of the past decade—Rwanda, Chechnya, East Timor, Sierra Leone, Bosnia, and Kosovo, among others—share one characteristic: they might have been prevented if the great nations of the world had possessed the political will to do so. Waiting to respond until tens of thousands of civilians have already lost their lives usually means that the most effective options for ending the crisis, including military responses, have been foreclosed. Political options that might have been possible before mass killings took place may well have been destroyed, along with those elements of society best able to make them work, and the use of force will have become greatly more dangerous to both combatants and civilians alike. The U.S. reluctance to incur casualties makes the deployment of those forces best able to suppress the violence—our own soldiers—even less likely once the civilian toll has mounted to many thousands.

The Rwanda genocide is one instance where the United States should have come to the aid of the victims and offered combat troops to defeat those carrying out the genocide once it had begun. Most observers believe that 5,000 well-trained and armed troops deployed promptly in early April 1994 could have done the job. Ironically, Rwanda is also a case where genocide could probably have been prevented or suppressed with no resort to American forces if the international community had been attentive to the warning signs of mass killing, had engaged in a campaign of intensive diplomatic and economic pressure against those responsible, and had bolstered U.N. forces in the country at the time. The Rwanda tragedy offers a number of lessons about what more might be done to prevent genocide or limit its scope.

INTELLIGENCE COLLECTION

Among the first tasks that your administration must address is the dearth of intelligence about mass killings. Intelligence agencies should be instructed to enhance collection of data that has bearing on genocide or mass killings, using all available resources including satellite imagery and radio and telephone intercepts. Intelligence and diplomatic personnel must scrutinize arms flows, the creation of civilian militia, the formation of mass grave sites, and the scapegoating of vulnerable political groups or ethnic minorities. A particular priority will be to identify those civilian and military leaders responsible for exacerbating ethnic tensions or commanding troops or militia who attack unarmed people. Human rights documentation based on interviews with victims for purposes of obtaining the fullest information on the perpetration of crimes and the identity of those responsible for them must be upgraded as well.

It is crucial that such intelligence data be disseminated so that a range of actors—within the U.S. government, among allies, and at the United Nations—can be alerted to the warning signs of potential genocide to come. It is worth noting that three months before the outbreak of mass killings in Rwanda, the U.S. Central Intelligence Agency (CIA) produced a classified intelligence report that genocide was being planned in Rwanda and predicting that half a million Tutsi Rwandans might lose their lives. But CIA reports that are ignored by policymakers are of no value in preventing genocide, and intelligence gathering alone is no substitute for action.

ACTIVIST, PREVENTIVE DIPLOMACY

Once it is clear that regimes or insurgencies are engaging in preparations for or actually carrying out mass killings, the State Department, the National Security Council (NSC), and, as necessary, the Defense Department should be tasked with developing aggressive diplomatic, political, and, on some occasions, military strategies aimed at compelling abusive regimes or murderous factions to end their crimes.

Appointing top-level point people within State, the NSC, and, as needed, Defense who are directly accountable to you for diplomatic, political, and military responses is crucial. Many of the U.S. government's past failings relate in part to red tape, bureaucratic torpor, and the absence of a decision-maker accountable for successful outcomes. During the Rwanda genocide, for example, once the Security Council took the decision, albeit belatedly, to bolster its tiny contingent of UNAMIR (United Nations Assistance Mission in Rwanda) peacekeepers with a force of African soldiers, armored vehicles for the troops were a necessity. The United States was the only military power with the capacity to provide and transport fifty armored personnel carriers to Rwanda with the speed required under circumstances of rapidly unfolding genocide. Laborious negotiations between the United Nations and the Pentagon, and bureaucratic tangles over the payment, the type, the color, and the location of the vehicles frittered away months while hundreds of thousands died, and eventually doomed the initiative altogether. The vehicles were never provided, the African force never deployed.

Business-as-usual bureaucracy is unacceptable when war criminals possess a ready supply of weapons and the level of organization that enable them to commit industrial levels of slaughter within days and weeks. Appointing senior officials to be accountable for planning and articulating rapid responses to mass abuses will help generate the urgency and alacrity within the U.S. government that such occasions require.

Among the diplomatic responses that should be considered are threatening perpetrators that if they fail to stop abuses they will be denounced by name, denied visas to travel, shunned, and shamed. The United States also should be prepared to recommend imposing economic sanctions (such as a suspension of World Bank and International Monetary Fund loans, debt negotiations, and foreign aid) if diplomacy and stigmatization are unsuccessful. These actions signal those in authority that their atrocities will not be tolerated, and on some occasions might encourage their domestic opponents to take action themselves to prevent further violations.

One of the most difficult challenges we will face is developing initiatives to curb abuses when the perpetrators are insurgent forces, not governments. As the Sierra Leone crisis demonstrated so vividly, diplomatic pressures were largely irrelevant to Foday Sankoh and the Revolutionary United Front he created and led, a monstrously abusive gang of drug-addicted, war-orphaned, diamond-stealing teenagers. But diplomatic pressures were not irrelevant to Liberian President Charles Taylor, Sankoh's chief ally in the region, whose own abusive regime recruited, trained, equipped, and supported the RUF throughout the civil war. If the United States, the United Kingdom, and African governments had made it clear to Taylor that he faced international sanctions, including a blockade on the diamonds he laundered for the insurgents, the RUF might not have developed militarily to the point that it could brutalize an entire nation. That pressure on Taylor, Sankoh, and the RUF would have been all the more effective if the international diamond industry, including the DeBeers consortium, had sent the message as well.

One area where diplomatic niceties need to be jettisoned is hate broadcasting. Radio was a crucial means of inciting Rwandans to murder their Tutsi neighbors. Terror television played a similar role in Bosnia, where Yugoslav President Slobodan Milosevic's propaganda apparatus filled the airwaves with hate-filled lies about the Bosnian Muslim minority and invited abuses against its members. If early-warning intelligence and human rights reports indicate that messages inciting ethnic hatred and murder are being broadcast on radio stations, and if diplomatic protests, condemnation, and appeals do not persuade the authorities to desist, the United States should be prepared to jam those broadcasts or provide others the means to disrupt them.

STRENGTHENING THE UNITED NATIONS

A crucial component of a new U.S. policy to prevent or stop crimes against humanity will be measures to sharpen the United Nations's ability to anticipate, prevent, and respond to them. At present, every U.N. function relevant to preventing or suppressing mass killings is inadequate. Nevertheless, the world is calling upon the United Nations to respond militarily in ever more conflict situations, especially those that disproportionately victimize civilians. The United Nations has deployed thirty-eight peacekeeping missions in the past twelve years—more than twice the number in the preceding forty years. Many of these initiatives have been extremely successful in terms of helping end wars that had grossly victimized civilians, such as in El Salvador and Mozambique. But the United Nations cannot be successful in peacekeeping if its forces are required either to accommodate or to disarm military forces who flout the terms of peace agreements, continue to engage in major violence, or are incorporated unrehabilitated into structures of power. As the crisis in Sierra Leone demonstrated, even operating under the mandate of U.N. authority, lightly armed battalions from developing-world armies are no solution when a peace agreement has been thoroughly violated and abusive forces are running rampant.

The best way to address this problem is for the United Nations, with American leadership, to create, train, equip, and fund a standing rapid-deployment force for the purpose of early intervention to thwart genocide and crimes against humanity. A relatively small, elite force from developed nations could respond quickly to human rights crises by subduing perpetrators of mass crimes, and creating the militarily permissive climate that is required for effective U.N. peacekeeping to take place. The U.S. Congress opposes any establishment of a standing force, and the bold step of doing so is not likely to be taken in the foreseeable future. Nonetheless, the failure by the international community to inhibit mass atrocities against civilians, especially the United Nations's humiliation in Sierra Leone, Bosnia, and Rwanda, demands that the United States and its allies make a concerted effort to move forward in establishing this essential capacity.

In the meantime, there are lesser measures that could improve considerably the United Nations's response to humanitarian and human rights crises. The secretary-general's special fund to deploy peacekeepers quickly in emergency situations is overdrawn and should be enlarged. Additionally, Congress should be urged to end its opposition to so-called standby troop arrangements. It is essential that the United Nations be permitted and empowered to move forward with plans for troop-contributing nations to pre-select, equip, and train military units that would be designated for U.N. interventions aimed at halting the types of atrocities described here. Ideally, such units would conduct regular military training exercises together under unified U.N. command. Preparing for such operations would not preclude a participating government from making specific decisions as specific cases arise. It would, however, enable those who choose to respond in a particular crisis to do so in a militarily proficient way.

Additional funding would also permit the U.N. secretariat to upgrade its military headquarters in New York, and to create and equip mobile headquarters with the capacity to direct operations in the field to protect civilians at risk. Independent intelligence-gathering capacity at U.N. command centers is especially needed. We should press Congress to appropriate the funds needed to designate and position armored vehicles and helicopters so that if international forces are required to respond quickly, the means to transport them will be in place. Acquiring the flexible capacity to intervene does not prejudge whether or not to do so. It does mean that once a decision to act has been made, it is more likely to be timely and effective.

The United States must reexamine its own contributions to coping with human rights disasters. The matter goes beyond payment of our peacekeeping dues to the United Nations, which is itself problematic, given Congress's refusal to fund the account fully and individual representatives' and senators' penchant for placing holds on the dispersal of appropriated funds. Enormous energy was devoted to persuading Congress to pay U.S. back dues to the United Nations. This administration will have to make a similar commitment of political resources. Additionally, however, the executive branch can itself respond with more generosity when emergency situations arise. The U.S. refusal when the secretary-general urgently requested a small number of rapid-reaction forces during the Sierra Leone hostage crisis was a low moment for American diplomacy, and the subsequent U.S. demand for prohibitively costly reimbursement for transporting U.N. troops to the scene compounded the negligence.

REGIONAL INTERVENTIONS

U.N. forces are not necessarily required in all instances where military force is needed. Regional political groupings can play a significant role in peacekeeping, and in some cases, peace enforcement and protection of civilians. The Nigerian role as leader of the Economic Community Monitoring Group (ECOMOG) in Sierra Leone prior to the 1999 Lome Accord, while marred by ECOMOG's own abuses against civilians, nonetheless kept the RUF insurgents at bay. For such regional or neighboring forces to play a larger role in defeating war criminals, they require a level of competence that most do not now possess. Stopping massive violence against unarmed victims requires the best elements of an army: those most expert in combat operations. All too often, the forces offered by troop-contributing countries to U.N. operations are not the crack battalions kept in the capital but the weakest, least professional units. When units with little combat experience find themselves in conflict situations opposite well-organized forces, they are unable to protect either the local population or themselves.

When coercive military force is required to subdue those engaged in mass killings of civilians, such operations require first- or second-world units with combat experience, backed by American or European-quality intelligence, logistics, transport, and communications. As part of our genocide prevention and response program, the United States should broaden its training and assistance to military forces from countries with decent, if not always democratic, governments. Your administration should as a matter of urgency begin now by identifying countries in proximity to situations where human rights abuses are running high. We should look for ways to aid friendly nations in identifying and training standby units for possible humanitarian intervention in the future.

POST-INTERVENTION RECONSTRUCTION

Neither American nor U.N. peacekeepers can provide lasting protection for vulnerable civilians forever. Suppressing those who are using the state's resources to commit vast crimes may well mean removing them from positions of responsibility in government, the army, and the police and, in some cases, expelling them from the geographic area altogether, as was the case in Kosovo and East Timor. But such actions create a vacuum of authority, one that the international community must, in collaboration with local civil society, fill as quickly and as effectively as possible. The aftermath of intervention to stop monstrous abuses can be even more difficult than the initial military endeavor. The United States and the great nations of the world can contribute collectively to keeping communities free of violence by helping them establish respectable police forces and judicial institutions.

One way to do so would be to upgrade financial support to the United Nations when it deploys foreign police forces to assist their local counterparts. Such endeavors have been crucial to preventing a return to abuses in such countries as El Salvador, Haiti, and

Bosnia. They have been remarkably less successful in Kosovo, in part because police-contributing countries have been slow to meet their obligations. In any case, enhanced funding for police assistance will help lighten the burden on the United Nations's blue helmets, or on our own or our allies' military forces.

ACCOUNTABILITY

Unless the perpetrators of genocide and crimes against humanity are apprehended and brought to justice, they will repeat their crimes and others will emulate them. Thus a program of preventing and responding to such crimes must also include a component for holding to account those responsible.

The United Nations, with strong support from the United States, created two international tribunals: one to judge and punish those responsible for the Rwanda genocide, the other for crimes against humanity in the former Yugoslavia. Since then, the United Nations has produced a treaty to create a standing court to bring to justice those responsible for crimes against humanity elsewhere, though it will be years before the International Criminal Court is fully operational.

In the meantime, there is no international tribunal or court to hold accountable those responsible for crimes in Sierra Leone, Afghanistan, Sudan, and elsewhere. The United States, in cooperation with the United Nations and its allies, must search for other ways to publicize the crimes that have been committed and stigmatize the perpetrators, both internationally and within their own societies. Political and financial support for formal, international commissions of inquiry are one important option. This mechanism was used very successfully in East Timor. Even though it was not associated with international prosecution of those Indonesian military officials responsible for atrocities, it was nonetheless remarkably useful in encouraging the Indonesian government itself to investigate and prosecute top army officials.

Accountability after the fact is not a substitute for interventions that save unarmed people from slaughter. In some cases, however, it may be all that is possible; thus it is all the more urgent that it be promoted and supported. In the case of massive Russian war operations in Chechnya in 1999 and 2000, for example, there was no possibility that the United Nations, the United States, or any other nation would engage in any form of military action that could have saved Chechen civilians from grossly abusive Russian troops. Even if there had been international will to protect Chechens, which was not in evidence, Russia's membership on the Security Council and its military and nuclear capabilities would have made intervention a practical impossibility.

There was an opportunity, however, at the height of Russian atrocities, to have created a formal commission of inquiry under U.N. auspices, during the March 2000 session of the U.N. Human Rights Commission. If the United States had not withheld political support, European governments were reportedly prepared to offer a resolution creating such a formal commission of inquiry into war crimes in Chechnya. That action might not have ended Russian atrocities, but it certainly would have raised the cost of indiscriminate military operations by embarrassing the government of President Vladimir Putin internationally. It also might have contributed, as similar action did in Indonesia, to national efforts to prosecute those who ordered military attacks upon civilians. A formal international investigation of Russian war crimes could have helped curtail them and deter their recurrence. It is a pity that the opportunity—along with a host of other diplomatic measures that might have been employed—was not seized.

CONCLUSION

In the real situations that pose questions of whether and how to intervene, no one will seriously advocate the automatic use of American military force. What is called for is a discriminating blend of measures that serve our moral purpose through pragmatic, proportionate application of the many tools at America's disposal. This is not an idealistic "no-man-is-an-island" rationale. It is a design for calculating U.S. interests on a truly comprehensive basis, recognizing that inaction in the face of such evils as we have seen in Rwanda, the Balkans, East Timor, and elsewhere undermines American leadership and invites their repetition elsewhere. Only vigorous, carefully calibrated intervention can stifle immediate abuses and deter others in the future.

It is vitally important that your administration demonstrate a commitment to oppose crimes against humanity wherever they occur, and to offer assistance to protect civilians and end abuses against them. That assistance need not be—and rarely will be—the introduction of U.S. troops. As this memo suggests, there are many policy alternatives to such measures, particularly if the U.S. government is serious about prevention. What must be reversed is the past pattern of American officials' repeatedly promising that the United States will never again tolerate genocide (or other forms of mass killings) and repeatedly failing to fulfill that promise. This administration can do better by articulating a doctrine that the prevention and suppression of genocide and crimes against humanity are a vital national interest, and offering appropriate resources to realize that commitment—diplomatically where possible, militarily where necessary and feasible.

MEMORANDUM TO THE PRESIDENT

Dov S. Zakheim

FROM: "The Secretary of Defense"

SUBJECT: Humanitarian Concerns Alone Do Not Justify Military Intervention

> "What is the United States national interest in Sierra Leone? There aren't any other than humanitarian interests."
>
> —Administration official who participated in the U.S. decision not to contribute to a rapid reaction force for Sierra Leone, quoted in the *New York Times,* May 10, 2000.

You have asked for my views regarding the proper policy that should govern military interventions for humanitarian purposes, and the circumstances in which such interventions might take place. It is my strong belief that other than in response to natural disasters, we should be exceedingly cautious about committing military forces of any kind to humanitarian operations. In those very limited cases where, having exhaustively searched for and applied non-military options, it is found that such commitments are absolutely unavoidable, they should nevertheless be limited to support functions. Only in the most extreme cases should the limited use of air strikes be considered, much less applied.

Thanks to CNN, CNBC, the BBC, and their counterparts, we have been led to believe that no longer can the leader of a great power pronounce any state to be, like Neville Chamberlain's Czechoslovakia, a far-off country about which we know little. Up-to-the-minute scenes from even the most exotic lands are beamed into our living rooms on a daily basis. The world seems to be separated from us by only a click of our TV remote control.

Our instant access to information anywhere has spawned a dangerous by-product, however: We are constantly at risk of committing our prestige, our resources, and indeed our lives to distant crises and conflicts because of the pressure, and at times the outrage, generated by televised scenes of those events. In fact, no responsible American, and particularly no president, should base policy simply on what is being shown on the evening news. That some have done so has created problems not only for them but for the American people as well.

Americans are a generous people with big hearts, always ready to look beyond their own concerns to those of other, less fortunate lands, but knee-jerk reaction to real-time reports of purported human rights abuses is often neither wise nor effective. An undisciplined proclivity to intervene indiscriminately in such cases will erode our capacity to intervene effectively in those cases where the combination of our interests and our values justifies doing so.

Often, indeed most of the time, the information that is beamed back to us on our television screens is at best incomplete and intermittent. The news media are highly selective, in terms of both where they go and what they show us. CNN and its counterparts only present what they are able to see for themselves. The television networks' inability to see much of what is happening in Chechnya does not mean that Russians are not butchering Chechens. Conversely, films of individual acts of cruelty in Kosovo do not in themselves point to murder on a massive scale. We must recognize that we cannot always and immediately assess those facts on the ground that at first blush seem to cry out for intervention.

Should we therefore never intervene abroad? Few will argue against interventions that are meant to fight the forces of nature. Our military has been at the forefront of humanitarian operations to help nations cope with the ravages of floods, fires, and famines. Deploying directly from their combat role in the Gulf War, U.S. Marines worked wonders in Bangladesh, fighting the floods of 1991 and, in concert with personnel from their sister services, providing food, water, and medical care to nearly two million people.

Marines also played a vital role in distributing food during our first Somalia intervention in 1992. Army units fought the massive outbreak of fires in Indonesia in 1997. In 1998, Seabees assisted the states of Central America in recovering from the devastating effects of Hurricane Mitch, as they did in Puerto Rico after Hurricane Hugo struck the following year. Most recently, in March 2000, American airmen in Joint Task Force Atlas Response worked hand-in-hand with nongovernmental organizations to provide relief to the flood victims of Mozambique. Just as our forces stand ready to help our own citizens when disaster strikes, so we will continue to be ready to help others who are desperate in the face of nature's force.

It is when the source of disaster is human force that the debate over "humanitarian" interventions must be joined. Ambiguity invariably surrounds either the circumstances wherein humans are the cause of death and destruction, or the context in which a response to such events might be mounted. In many ways it was the Holocaust that spurred today's imperative inclination to rescue victims of official violence or civil strife. Yet John McCloy, the official who blocked the order to bomb the railway tracks leading to Auschwitz, went to his grave believing that the opportunity cost of diverting aircraft to that mission was too high a price to pay as the war effort reached its culmination.

It is true that McCloy's decision has since been universally rejected. It has become an article of faith that the world will not tolerate another Holocaust. Indeed, the memory of the Holocaust contributed in some small part to the American decision during the Gulf War to divert tactical aviation assets to hunt for Scuds missiles, a decision that was opposed by General Norman Schwarzkopf on grounds analogous to those that McCloy had invoked. The United States simply was not prepared to stand by as Holocaust survivors in Israel were targeted by missiles that might be carrying warheads with poison gas.

Both the bombings that did not take place in World War II and those that were directed against the Scuds in the Gulf War involved the redirection of relatively limited assets in wartime in response to an unambiguous threat to civilians. In neither instance was there a call for the introduction of American ground troops. In most cases of humanitarian intervention, the issue is whether to commit assets, especially combat forces, in the first place. That issue is clouded by a far greater degree of ambiguity and is therefore much more likely to prompt opposition from our military policymakers and leaders. There is a price to be paid whenever American forces intervene in any situation that involves the potential of confronting hostile fire. That price has both a measurable and an unmeasurable component. The component that can be measured in dollars involves the expenditure of materiel of various kinds, from the large weapons system like the F-117 that was brought down over Serbia to the smallest-caliber shell. The component that is not measurable, and is of infinitely greater importance, is the cost of human life, the cost of even one American soldier, sailor, airman, or Marine, whose future will be lost, and whose family will mourn. To put the issue in its starkest terms, the cause must not only be worth killing for, it must be worth dying for.

American forces are expected to lay down their lives for their country. They must be prepared to accept that the term "their country" means their country's interests, as defined by the nation's duly elected civilian leadership. Absent any strategic American interest, should Americans still be expected to die in uniform?

This question haunts the debate over humanitarian interventions. Are Americans dying so that others might live? Or so that they might thrive? There is surely a difference between the two. The former offers a far more compelling case for intervention than the latter. Yet, in the heat of a crisis, or indeed of a conflict, it is not at all clear which of the two—a better life or life itself—is really at risk.

Kosovo and Bosnia provide good examples of this dilemma. No doubt ethnic cleansing was taking place in both places. There were, as well, numerous atrocities. Yet in hindsight it has been learned that the atrocities were not as widespread as has been assumed, and that ethnic cleansing really involved mainly the displacement of people from their homes. Such behavior is no trifling matter, but it is not mass murder. It debases the term "genocide" to apply it to these cases.

The hindsight that allowed observers to conclude that the scope of the atrocities was smaller than originally believed developed only after a not insignificant time lag, one of months rather than weeks. We must always take such a time lag into account. Doing so should not be an excuse for inaction where action is necessary, but it should enable us to have a clear understanding of the real stakes involved in any action that we might take.

States are often confronted with reports of atrocities that ultimately prove to have been exaggerated. At times those reports are generated by one of the combatant parties in order to shore up domestic support for its cause. For example, stories of German atrocities in Belgium helped to galvanize the British public's support for its government's policies during the early stages of World War I.

At other times reports that horrify their recipients are furnished by whatever side wishes to prompt an intervention by an outside power. That clearly was the case in Kosovo. The number of ethnic Albanians killed by Serb irregulars was considerably lower than what initially had been reported to the American public.

We should not lightly dismiss what actually may have taken place in any of the foregoing cases. We must at the same time, however, recognize that exaggeration and sometimes outright deception on the part of participants on both sides magnifies the natural ambiguity and uncertainty that inevitably clouds what actually is happening on the ground.

Television, ever geared to instant analysis governed by the sound-bite, will rarely, if ever, be in a position to verify reports of atrocities. Such verification involves painstaking research, and research takes time, which for television in particular is always in short supply. To emphasize the importance of careful assessment of atrocity reports is not to counsel indifference. It is, rather, the prudent political equivalent of the Hippocratic oath. Intervention, like a medical operation, involves costs, risks, and in most cases blood. Government needs to determine the nature and extent of the illness before it cuts into the patient.

Some might make the case that atrocities need not be the only trigger for an American intervention. They can reasonably contend that displacing hundreds of thousands of people—what really happened in Kosovo—should have been enough to trigger the deployment of military force, even if there were few atrocities and murders committed by Serbs against Albanians.

Yet the United States has been exceedingly selective about intervening when people have been displaced and even when they have been butchered. The slaughter of over half a million Rwandans in the spring and summer of 1994 was insufficient to prompt more than a token military gesture on the part of the United States. Russia has decimated every major and minor population center in Chechnya, creating thousands of internal refugees. The United States has not intervened. There have been large movements of people in Sudan, as a result of the interminable fighting in that miserable country. The United States has not intervened. There have been major population movements out of East Timor. The United States did not intervene, other than to support the efforts of others, notably Australia. Over a million souls are homeless in the Democratic Republic of the Congo, displaced as a result of the brutal, seemingly endless tribal warfare that has permeated the Great Lakes region. The United States has not intervened. We must face up to the plain fact that during most of the past decade America pursued a policy that most accurately could be termed "selective humanitarian intervention."

Especially in the latter part of the 1990s, American policymakers were quick to rationalize their nonintervention. Russia was too powerful. Rwanda and the Congo were too remote. Sudan was too complicated. Timor was somebody else's problem.

Yet if it is worth risking an American life for a displaced Kosovar, why not a displaced Tutsi, Chechen, or southern Sudanese? Indeed, if it is worth risking an American life for the life of a Kosovar, is that of a Tutsi, Chechen, or southern Sudanese worth any less? On the other hand, if we believe that we cannot intervene in every humanitarian crisis, are we not choosing among competing crises, deciding when exactly we should intervene and when we need not do so?

The undeniable fact is that in recent years our choices have had less to do with the merits of any given crisis than we have been prepared to admit. We have been quick to bully smaller states, whether with cruise missiles that hit Sudan and Afghanistan, or high-altitude bombers that hit Serbia, but we have not been prepared to pick on someone close to our own size, like Russia when it razes

Chechnya. "Intervene in Kosovo," we were told, because its fortunes will affect European stability. Yet no one tendered similar counsel to intervene against a destabilizing implosion inside Russia. To continue in this vein does not resolve the basic question of whether we should intervene at all when confronting a humanitarian crisis.

Advocates of intervention argue that doing so will somehow deter others from attempting ethnic cleansing or worse. They fail to acknowledge the fundamental difference between a credible threat designed to deter one state from attacking another and the far less convincing threat to attack a state for its behavior inside its own borders.

Let us be honest with ourselves. The criteria for intervention have had less to do with the nature of any particular humanitarian crisis than with much more mundane concerns such as power balances, state interests, and military feasibility. Those factors have defined the context in which the humanitarian cause is invariably placed. Yet the U.S. government's past misplaced rhetoric, its inconsistency regarding its declaratory criteria for intervention, and its unwillingness explicitly to acknowledge those factors that led it to intervene selectively in humanitarian crises have seriously undermined, and called into question, the viability of the very policy it was publicly committed to pursue.

For the government to argue that those humanitarian interventions that it authorized were in America's interest, while those that it did not were not in that interest, was, to put it mildly, disingenuous. Why was protecting Somalis more in America's interest than protecting Sudanese? Why was aiding America's allies in Europe more important to America's interests than aiding our ally Australia in East Timor? Unfortunately, we became captives of our own hyperbole and failed to recognize that other "hype"—hypocrisy—that colors and distorts our actions.

Finally, we consistently overlooked the reality that what we might initially have anticipated as a short-term, "limited engagement" could be regarded as an existential threat by those whom we attacked. Whether it be Milosevic's Yugoslavia or Saddam Hussein's Iraq (or indeed, Ho Chi Minh's Vietnam), the will to survive, even if defeated on the battlefield, could force the United States into a military commitment measured in years, not weeks, and in tens of billions, not millions, of dollars. It is time we became serious about what interventions can and cannot do, when they should be pursued, and what their consequences are likely to be.

First we must recognize that military interventions, however justified they might appear to be, are always a grim business. The use of force invariably leads to death and destruction, yet its results are frequently problematical. In other words, there will always be some harm to someone when force is used, but there might be no good for anyone as a result.

We as a nation are blessed with a short historical memory that is the by-product of our eternal optimism. We forget our failures. We forget the damage that those failures have left in their wake. Those failures span several administrations. The failed mission in Lebanon in 1982 through 1984, the failed interventions in Somalia between 1993 and 1994, the failed intervention in Haiti in 1994, and the botched attempt to organize a Kurdish resistance in Iraq in 1991 and again in 1996 did not take place in a vacuum. In each case the consequences damaged our interests and those whom we sought to aid.

Our withdrawal from Lebanon complicated our difficulties in the Arab world and did not bring an end to the bloody Lebanese civil war. To this day that unhappy country remains a vassal of Syria, with over 40,000 Syrian troops still deployed on its soil.

Retreating from our second intervention in Somalia left that benighted country in the hands of bands of thugs and undermined the system for distributing food to the needy that our initial intervention had put in place. We even damaged our relations with the United Nations, though it was in the name of the United Nations that we had organized the intervention in the first place.

Our withdrawal from Haiti left that impoverished place in the hands of the same elites that had exploited the general populace for decades. We did not restore democracy, as we had promised we would, and once again we sent a message to our neighbors that we would violate their sovereignty when it suited us.

Our inept gestures of support for the Iraqi resistance to Saddam's predations is the latest in a long series of American betrayals of Kurdish freedom fighters, beginning with Woodrow Wilson's broken promise of Kurdish independence during the Versailles peace talks. Saddam has tightened his grip on the ground in northern Iraq even as our forces control the skies above.

Tragically, our interventions in southeastern Europe likewise have been of dubious utility. Our vision of a multi-ethnic society, with groups that have hated each other for generations somehow living side by side, has blinded us to the reality that even the presence of our forces, and those of our allies, has not prevented more blood from being spilled. On our present course we are doomed to remain in the Bosnian briar patch for another generation, and in Kosovo for perhaps even longer. Albanians will not soon forgive the ethnic cleansing that Belgrade inflicted on them. Nor will Serbs forget that we did little to prevent the displacement of their brethren by Croatia in 1999, or that our de facto occupation of Kosovo has neither prevented ethnic Albanians from murder and mayhem, nor restrained some Kosovar fighters from moving their operations to other parts of Serbia.

Each of these interventions left death and destruction in its wake. Nearly 300 Americans died in Lebanon, as did countless more Lebanese. Thirty of our soldiers died in Somalia, some being brutally dragged through the streets of Mogadishu. Hundreds of other Somalis died as a result of the tribal warfare that we did not, and could not, stop, much less prevent. Our Kosovo operation produced hundreds of innocent victims throughout Serbia, casualties of imprecision that even the most scrupulous targeting cannot avoid. Millions more suffer the cruelties of an economy reduced to third-world status by the devastation of its infrastructure. One mistake, the bombing of the Chinese embassy in Belgrade, complicated our relations with China at a time when those relations were fragile at best.

Second, we must admit to ourselves that our interventions serve no deterrent purpose whatsoever. Each group involved in some form of ethnic strife not only nurses deep-seated grievances but believes that its own case, and cause, is sui generis. "You don't understand," that old refrain of white South Africans when questioned about apartheid, is the stock-in-trade answer of radical Serbs, Croats, Albanians, Northern Irish Catholics and Protestants, Palestinians, Israelis, Hutus, Tutsis, and all the rest.

Indeed, even in the unlikely event that these groups might acknowledge that their situation parallels those of others, they still would not be deterred from pursuing their cause by violent means. What exactly would deter them? Our failure to put an end to those civil conflicts in which we did intervene? Saddam's survival? Or his slow recovery of northern Iraq? Milosevic's ongoing machinations in Kosovo? Or the Albanians' reported new designs on other parts of Serbia? Ongoing tribal warfare in Somalia? Continuing political and economic oppression in Haiti?

Third, we should recognize that there is what economists call an "opportunity cost" to our interventions. When we deploy our troops overseas to intervene in humanitarian crises we deprive them of opportunities to train for their primary mission, which is to fight and defeat a major American adversary. Indeed, in deploying our forces on humanitarian operations we always run the risk that they will be unavailable for timely deployment to a major theater of combat. We therefore run the risk of adding to battlefield casualties due to insufficient training, inadequate reinforcement, or both.

Fourth, we should come to grips with another basic fact: the damage that our interventions can cause is not merely human and material. It is also legal and, paradoxically, moral as well. The principle that national sovereignty is inviolable has underpinned international behavior since the Treaty of Westphalia in 1648. It was because that principle was violated that Britain and France went to war with Nazi Germany in 1939, and that we joined them two years later. It was on the basis of that principle that we rushed to the side of the Republic of Korea in 1950, and did the same for Kuwait four decades later. To violate a nation's sovereignty, when the specific legal and constitutional conditions that attach to the term "genocide" have not been met, and especially when it is clear that genocide even in its nontechnical sense is not an issue, as it was not in Kosovo, is to threaten to unravel the entire fabric of international relations. It is to undermine the justification for

America's support for its friends around the globe. It is to invite state-sponsored lawlessness and anarchy on an international scale.

Fifth, we must admit that when America's interests are not directly involved and understandable to our citizenry, our national attention span is short. In the absence of a compelling and durable national interest, congressional patience with overseas operations may be even shorter. Since the dismal chapter in American history that was the war in Vietnam, Congress has been far more skeptical about American interventions abroad. In prosecuting Operation Desert Storm to defeat Iraqi aggression in a region of grave importance to the world economy, strong congressional reservations were overcome only after a close Senate vote. In particular, when an administration cannot clearly articulate why America should engage its forces overseas, Congress becomes increasingly likely to place restraints upon the nature and duration of deployments. This is a fact of public life, not of partisan politics. A Democratic administration withdrew its forces from Somalia in 1994 under pressure from a Democratic Congress.

We are fond of calling the past hundred years "the American century," but we should beware of hubris. Our power is not unlimited, neither are our resources. Nor should we delude ourselves that our values are easily exportable.

Impulsive intervention is rarely judicious. Demands for quick intervention in what we may perceive as a humanitarian crisis must be gauged not only against our desire to help, but against the most careful analysis of whether in the long term hasty military action will do more good than harm. It was an error of omission when our bombers did not attack the rail lines to Auschwitz in 1945, but it was an error of commission when our bombers attacked convoys inside Kosovo some five decades later. The latter error bound us to do great harm directly to thousands and indirectly to millions in that province and elsewhere in the Balkans, without any confident expectation of lasting benefit.

We must also recognize that it is pointless to intervene in order to make those whose historical memories are much longer than ours forget the grievances that they have nursed for so many years. We certainly understand that we cannot get Israelis and

Palestinians to bury their memories and live together in harmony. Indeed, we have worked for years to enable them to live separately in harmony. We know that we cannot get Indians and Pakistanis to forget that they have fought three bitter wars since their independence from Britain. We have not yet recognized that our military presence in southeastern Europe will not get Serbs to forget their massive displacement by the Croats in 1993, or their persecution by the Ustashe fifty years earlier, or their current victimization by ethnic Albanians. Nor will we convince Kosovar Albanians to forget Milosevic's legacy, or to abandon their attempts to enlarge their sphere of influence in order to achieve the greater Albania of their dreams.

Americans tend to bank on the rationality of others. We convince ourselves that their grievances can be resolved through reasoned argument and compromise. But embittered people, who view history through the prisms of their misfortunes, are anything but rational. It does not matter a whit to a Serb what really happened on the Field of Ravens in 1389. It is what that Serb believes happened that matters. Nor does it matter that greater Albania, like so many other irredentist preoccupations, is nothing more than a fantasy. It is a fantasy that animates Albanians to violent rebellion—and frightens their neighbors into comparably violent countermeasures.

Beliefs function in a realm that reason cannot enter. Sometimes those beliefs, and the grievances real and imagined that often accompany them, can be overcome. The prejudices that are the unhappy by-product of both may yield to education and experience, but only in time frames that far exceed those that the partisans of humanitarian interventions appear to contemplate.

We too harbor beliefs. We believe that democracy is so manifestly in the interests of humankind anywhere, and that our brand of multi-ethnic democracy in particular carries with it a special attraction, that it is easily exportable to states with no democratic tradition of any kind. We forget that our democracy was not built in a day, that for the better part of a century after our independence we tolerated slavery in our midst, that the precious right to vote was granted to all citizens only in the previous century, and that it was only within our lifetime that it became meaningful for the descendants of slaves.

Moreover, individuals came to America from the world over to leave behind the legacies of hatred that sullied their homelands. They sought the opportunity that can best flourish when bigotry and bias are absent or repudiated. Yet America itself has not fully realized their dream. No one will argue that our society has rid itself of the scourge of prejudice.

Yet proclaiming and pursuing that ideal did make this country unique. With the passage of time we have learned not to give vent to prejudice with violence, to punish those who do, and to protect the targets of violence fueled by such prejudice. America's uniqueness is, by definition, not easily imitated. It certainly cannot be forced down the throats of those unwilling to emulate us, no matter how long our forces patrol the streets of their cities and towns. We can, and should, lead by example—ours is a successful multi-ethnic and multiracial society—but we must allow time for that example to sink in. Different groups in different circumstances will absorb the lessons of tolerance and mutual respect in different ways and at different rates.

To counsel a careful calculus of interests when deciding upon intervention is not to forswear intervention entirely. We must remain ever vigilant to the threat of genocide. As the world's leading democracy, America cannot stand by if one group of people attempts to exterminate another. Passivity in the face of genocide would undermine our very sense of who we are as a nation. We could not be, as John Quincy Adams put it, "a beacon to the world." Our light would dim. We could not rally others to the cause of a just order among nations.

The requirement not to be passive is not necessarily synonymous with the need to commit forces, however. In dealing with perceived acts of genocide, America has available to it a ladder of escalating responses that fall short of military intervention, but that, if applied in timely fashion, could be equally, indeed more, effective. A case in point is Rwanda, where the United States not only did not intervene but used its seat on the Security Council to forestall others from doing so. Washington could and should have warned the Rwandan authorities that it would not tolerate ethnic killings; it did so only sotto voce. It could have suspended aid. It did not do so. It could have jammed Rwandan hate radio. It did not do so. It could have supported an increase in the U.N. force on the ground—those forces did not include American troops—and mandated that force to seize weapons used in the killings. It did not do so.

Would there have been genocide had any or all of the foregoing steps been taken? Possibly. But its likelihood would have been far lower. The issue was therefore one not of troop deployments, but of timely and coherent responses to developments that were manifest to all who bothered to pay attention to them. The deployment of American forces should not provide a cover-up for an American policy vacuum.

What applies in the case of genocide applies even more in other instances, including those of crimes against humanity. In such cases, we must look to those whose interests are most directly affected to take the lead. It is for them to take the lion's share of responsibility for protecting one group of adversaries in civil strife from the predations of another. We should take careful note of Operation Alba, the Italian-led intervention by the Western European Union in Albania that stopped the tribal killings in that country. The United States stood on the sidelines; those with the most immediate and greatest interest in regional stability stepped up to the task at hand.

There will be cases where logistics and the absence of intelligence limit the ability of our allies to deal with crimes against humanity and other, lesser, but still urgent humanitarian crises. In those circumstances, we should draw upon our comparative advantage in military capability to support those of our friends who can benefit from it in quelling egregious affronts to human safety. No one can match our airlift, our command and control, our intelligence and reconnaissance resources. Those of our friends who need that support should not doubt that they will receive it when they protect interests that, while vital to them, are common to us both. Nevertheless, as our more recent support of Australian forces in East Timor, and our airlift of French, Moroccan, and Tunisian troops in the Shaba crises of the 1970s both demonstrated, our commitment of logistics and other forms of support to our allies need not escalate into a deployment of combat forces.

Certainly, we put at risk the lives of those who will provide support to friendly combat forces that intervene in humanitarian crises. Nevertheless, that risk will be lower than the risk attaching to front-line duty. Moreover, the risk would be commensurate with our primary interest in maintaining the cohesion of our alliances, rather than in resolving internal conflicts that do not significantly affect American security or well-being.

As we contribute to the operations of our friends and allies, we must do one more thing: We must be more willing to cede command responsibility to our allies. It is simply wrong-headed to commit large numbers of American forces in order to obtain command of an interventionary exercise that is not properly ours to pursue. Our contribution and our command responsibility should be commensurate with our stakes in the contingency in question. No more, no less.

America's resources are not unlimited; neither is its prescience or its moral authority. We must husband all three. Because of our technological prowess and economic might, only the United States can remain fully prepared to combat major interstate aggression. If we are to do so, however, we cannot squander our resources acting as the cop on every beat and intervening in every squabble.

It will serve neither ourselves nor our allies, nor the larger goal of a just international order, if we permit U.S. forces to be exhausted by endless deployments. Moreover, whenever Americans are committed to military intervention, whether directly or in support of other forces, they must understand why their mission is important to the security of the country they serve and for which they are ready to die. We must not confuse our personnel by deploying them on missions for which they have not trained, or, worse still, training them for missions that are not central to their primary responsibilities on the battlefield.

America's wider responsibilities require us to husband the tactical and theater support infrastructure that would be critical to the prosecution of a major conflict. It makes no sense to expend critical spare parts or wear out our systems on deployments and missions that other states could prosecute equally effectively.

The latest involvement in Kosovo teaches a lesson we should long since have learned. The costs of deployments are habitually underestimated by policymakers and invariably run into the billions of dollars. Exceptional expenses of that magnitude cannot be sustained by shifting funds from our already overtaxed acquisition accounts. America achieved its current military prowess thanks to investments and research that were funded in the 1980s. Without ongoing investments, our forces will decline in both quality and quantity. Our comparative military advantage will erode. We will not be able to come to the aid of others, as we did during 1990 and 1991, when aggression was naked and unambiguous.

Most of all, we should refrain from framing generalized doctrines that are honored more in the breach than in practice. We should not let our friends and allies believe that we are a crutch upon which they can lean when their interests, whether strategic or even moral, are more at stake than ours. We should avoid making promises that mislead ethnic groups into believing that we will rush to their side. Creating expectations of American intervention is more likely to exacerbate crises than to calm them. That is a moral hazard that statesmen should avoid.

We cannot be all things to all people, but we can be true to ourselves. American leaders must preserve our sense of priorities and of national purpose. That dictates military intervention overseas only when our own interests are clearly at stake, or when genocide is so manifest that refusal to act would destroy our moral leadership of the free world. Only by speaking and acting with prudence and restraint will we preserve the credibility upon which world peace and international stability continue to depend.

MEMORANDUM TO THE PRESIDENT

Stanley A. McChrystal

FROM: "Chairman, Joint Chiefs of Staff"

SUBJECT: A Balanced Policy on Humanitarian Intervention

Mr. President, a realistic policy on humanitarian intervention is required. Our experiences in Somalia, Haiti, Bosnia, and Kosovo have shown us the absolute need to develop clear guidelines regarding the use of American military forces in humanitarian interventions. Political and legal considerations, moral imperatives, and practical military limitations must all be weighed to produce a realistic, workable framework for national decision-making. While retaining some flexibility, that policy must also provide international actors with clearly understood American interests and positions on humanitarian issues.

The time to develop our policy is now, before the next crisis appears. We must come to grips with what is important to us, and what price we are prepared to pay for our interests and values. We must do it before television cameras capture the next round of sad images and vocal interests raise a cacophony of calls for action. It should be in place before we attend the next late-night meeting in your office when time is short and philosophical thought seems out of place. Then we must steer by that policy when emotions run high.

Before we attempt to define this critical policy, we must recognize the grave implications of our task. We should review the record of past efforts and understand our successes and failures. We should know of the many lives our interventions have saved, and the many they have cost. We should go to Arlington, where you have spoken often of fallen heroes, and there on the hillside ask ourselves what we are willing to have our young die for.

A viable policy on humanitarian intervention must be based on a realistic evaluation of the strategic environment in which we operate, it must follow overarching principles that accurately represent American values, and it must include specific criteria against which emerging situations can be evaluated. The decision to commit our forces must be the result of a thought-out policy executed through a rigorous, disciplined decision-making process. As we have learned bitterly in the past, the potential costs demand nothing less.

As your senior military adviser, I believe that failure to produce such a policy will endanger our position of leadership in the world while continuing to overburden our limited military forces. We must not put at risk our military capability to perform core missions crucial to national defense.

THE NEED FOR BALANCE

The policy must be one of balance. Intervention is serious business, and for both practical and moral reasons, the policy we formulate must be one that carefully weighs risks, benefits, and responsibilities. Extremes of idealistic interventionism or complete isolationism are equally impractical and incongruent with our foreign policy requirements and national character.

We must recognize several imperatives. It is self-evident that when vital or strategic national interests are at stake, if we have the means, we will intervene. Our record there is clear, but it must also be apparent that in the face of a terrible evil such as genocide, America, preferably in concert with its allies but alone if need be, will intervene to save lives and reduce suffering.

However, we must also recognize that the self-evident cases are likely to be rare. Few situations offer such recognizable extremes and undeniable rationale for employing military force as vital national interests or genocide. Information is often incomplete or suspect, and in the absence of unequivocal imperatives the decision becomes more difficult—a complex calculus of practical and moral considerations. This is where our policy must be crafted with utmost care.

The root issue for policy is what weight, or value, we assign to humanitarian considerations when making decisions to intervene militarily. The extent to which we allow humanitarian considerations to move us to intervene and the threshold of suffering or evil we set as a precipitant for our intervention are the underlying factors that will always drive our decision-making in fluid, ambiguous situations. Examining and clarifying our own thinking on these factors, before a crisis, is essential.

It is military reality that the nation is incapable of unlimited action around the world. It is political reality that unconstrained or poorly justified U.S. military intervention would be neither supported nor accepted, either by Congress or by other nations. But it is a moral reality that the values of the nation and our position of world leadership will continue to provide a powerful impetus to use American force in meeting humanitarian crises.

American military intervention must therefore be strongly justified by recognized U.S. strategic interests, internationally accepted humanitarian criteria, or a reasonable combination of the two. The basic priorities of national survival dictate that elements of American power be directed first toward vital interests and only after that toward everything else, including humanitarian interventions.

So first of all our policy on intervention must be prudent. Neither a policy of overly idealistic, energetic intervention nor one of risk-averse isolationism is right for America. The former risks our strength and resources; the latter, our soul. America's policy must strike a balance in which neither our values nor our strategic interests are ignored. It must be a responsible balance that reflects our importance to the world.

KEY ASPECTS OF THE STRATEGIC ENVIRONMENT

Determining the appropriate calculus for American intervention demands that we understand key aspects of the strategic environment that will frame any decision to commit U.S. forces.

Imagery: The Pressure to Intervene

We live in a world of images and their effect upon us is profound. We are assailed with pictures of brutal war in Chechnya, horrific atrocities by seemingly irrational combatants in Sierra Leone, ethnic cleansing in Bosnia and Kosovo, starvation in the Sudan, and genocide in Rwanda. These are powerful images that shock, sadden, and often anger us.

Most Americans also possess personal images that are private, sacred, and equally powerful. America's collective memory of oppression and brutality—stories of cruel slavery, political oppression, war, and the horror that was the Holocaust—do much to define Americans as individuals and to mold who we are as a people. Those images, public and private, strike a chord that calls us to action— action to feed the hungry, protect the weak, and provide hope to those whose lives seem hopeless. It can and does produce tremendous pressure to intervene.

This pressure is predictable and in line with our history and national character. Our history reflects an idealism, generosity, and a willingness to sacrifice for others, from our own Civil War to the Marshall Plan, that have given us a place of respect and honor in the hearts of men and women around the world. It is a reputation we have earned through our efforts for others, and it is a national quality that we must nurture and protect.

We must, however, remember that images cut both ways. As stories of suffering or injustice call us to intervene, images such as pictures of young Americans and Somalis dead in the streets of Mogadishu or the unintended civilian casualties that accompany every conflict act as powerful counterforces. We must keep both images in mind, tempering our desire to help and willingness to sacrifice with a realism born of experience. We do well to remember that for every monument erected by the grateful citizens of a nation we have aided, there are countless graves in Arlington and other hallowed ground marking our sacrifices in failed or fruitless efforts. Intervention is never easy and, regardless of the price paid, is often ultimately futile. Failure in ill-considered actions can produce their own images that drive us inward. Those images can haunt future, more pressing tragedies, preventing our needed intervention. There is fodder enough for those who would recoil from the terrible costs of intervening to help others. We must use our maturity and judgment to prevent the power of images from controlling our policy.

The World: Protecting Progress

The heart-wrenching visions of war, injustice, and suffering we see so often today make us question whether true progress among people and nations is possible. Despite the reality of those tragedies, we must remember that the world today is largely a story of success.

World economic growth, bringing dramatic improvements in nutrition, health, education, and hope, continues to transform our future potential. Hunger persists, but we have essentially proven Malthus wrong.

Tangible material progress has gone hand in hand with political progress. The retreat from fascism and communism has given more people than ever before the freedom to express their thoughts and exercise true power through the ballot box. Increasingly, national and international laws are protecting the rights and property of nations, businesses, and individuals. Properly developed, structures like the International Criminal Court offer hope for even greater progress in taming abuses of human rights and human beings.

Without question, international stability is central to the advances that have benefited the world generally, and the United States specifically. Organizations and relationships based on trust, morality, and law are the pillars of a just world order.

In trade alone, the effects of globalization have been monumental. Agreements such as the North American Free Trade Agreement (NAFTA) and organizations such as the European Union (EU), the World Trade Organization, and the International Monetary Fund deepen the interdependence of groups and governments. Millions of workers in every corner of the globe owe their jobs and opportunities to these rapidly growing systems.

The United Nations, while still far from perfect, is a forum for vigorous debate and, increasingly, a force for collective action.

Combined with NATO, the EU, and other structures, we are capable of joining together to tackle difficult problems once thought insoluble.

Mr. President, the "so what" of all of this is that while tremendous problems, injustices, and tragedies persist in the world, progress has been rapid, and the pace appears to be increasing. But it can also be fragile. We share with other nations a grave responsibility to address great wrongs in the world, but we must guard against the impatience or self-righteousness that might deny countries the chance to develop normally, or create more pain and suffering than the wrong we sought to address.

America: The Implications of Unprecedented Power

America's unique position defines our role, our options, and our responsibilities. Our economic might, cultural influence, and recognized leadership are unprecedented.

Military power, long a primary measure of national power, is still a basic factor in a world where force and violence are common. In this arena, despite huge post–Cold War cutbacks, America is preeminent. We boast an impressively professional military, one steeped in the concept of selfless service and civilian control and, as demonstrated during the Gulf War and Kosovo, the most technologically advanced and lethal force in history. No other nation can currently challenge us, and our ability to deter as well as defeat potential enemies is a cornerstone of stability.

American leadership, accepted with hesitation only during the last century, has established a new standard for the benevolent use of power. We are the nation to which other countries look first for assistance, for action, for support. To us often falls the task of mobilizing the power of other nations to leverage our own potential for good. Without U.S. political engagement, conflicts in the Balkans, the Middle East, and Ireland would have burned longer and fiercer than they have.

The extent of our power offers a unique opportunity to serve the cause of human rights and international reconciliation. Often, it is only the United States that can rally nations and apply power where action is needed. We must be prepared, when circumstances warrant, to pay the price, sometimes for purely humanitarian causes. We must, however, match our willingness with wisdom. Each action must follow a sober appraisal of the situation. No simple, single prescription covers all humanitarian calamities. The unavoidable task for American statecraft is to judge whether, when, and how to meet each particular calamity.

The Need For Periodic Action and Constant Strength

Our military strength, alone or as part of a coalition, is fundamental to any policy we pursue on humanitarian intervention. It often defines our options, and an understanding of what it must address is essential.

Our requirement is one of periodic action, but constant strength. We must possess the ability at any time to project credible force and back it with political will. Perhaps more important, our constant strength and resolve serve as a deterrent, an insurance policy, and a significant source of critical stability across a wide range of situations.

Some situations require continuing vigilance. States such as North Korea and Iraq pose a persistent threat of major conflict, against which only acknowledged strength and unequivocal commitment can maintain the peace. Terrorism, capped by the nightmare of potential weapons of mass destruction, demands unflagging attention and unwavering resolve.

Others require rapid action and selfless sacrifice. Natural disasters place straightforward claims on our assistance. The scope of damage and suffering seen in tragedies such as the earthquake in Turkey in 1999 or the devastation wrought by Hurricane Mitch in Central America in 1998 demands massive, expensive, and often long-term relief. Catastrophes of those types are not the main challenge to policy; disasters wrought by human beings are. Wars are acts of men, not of nature; they are almost always less clear-cut, but they can demand the same willingness to act swiftly and potently. Saddam Hussein's conquest of Kuwait in 1990 was reversed only by an immediate movement of allied forces, while the failure of outside forces to prevent, or even reduce, the genocide in Rwanda in 1994 illustrates the possible costs of failing to act.

Still other cases require not direct military intervention, but determined, patient diplomatic leadership. Progress in the Mideast peace process, nuclear nonproliferation, the prevention or solution of regional conflicts such as that between India and Pakistan, reducing human rights abuses—these objectives demand more subtle measures than direct military action. In some circumstances American military power must still cast its shadow over regional adversaries; to prevent situations requiring military intervention, the prudent U.S. policy may be to shore up security arrangements among potential combatants, aiming to discourage their resort to violence. Our policy must integrate not only the use of American military power for humanitarian interventions but its conservation and maintenance as well.

A FRAMEWORK FOR DECISION-MAKING

The strategic environment in which we live and our role as sole superpower give special importance to our policy for humanitarian intervention and to the process we employ in implementing it. That process must be straightforward but will never be simple. It must begin with understanding exactly what problem we're facing.

Defining the Problem and the Objective
The first step is obvious, absolutely critical, and often done poorly or not at all. We must understand the problem, normally complex, and what outcome we really want. For an impatient nation, often ignorant of the past and enamored with quick solutions, this has historically been a significant problem for us.

We entered Vietnam with two major miscalculations: a Cold War view of a war of national liberation and a poor appraisal of the ability of the South Vietnamese government to establish legitimacy with its people. As a result we built a ten-year commitment on an unstable foundation—only to watch it collapse.

From 1982 to 1984 our Marines in Lebanon pursued policy objectives that were murky at best, and those objectives proved dubious indeed when that deadly conflict exacted such a heavy toll on our troops' lives.

Somalia began with a rush to feed a starving population and evolved, with little apparent consideration or debate, into open combat with the warring clans. Only after a battle in which eighteen Americans and hundreds of Somalis died did we consider what price we were willing to pay in order to reach a goal we couldn't really specify.

Then Haiti, and now the Balkans. We must force ourselves to identify the exact problem we are attempting to address and whether or not we can actually solve or even reduce it. Then we should take the estimated costs and double them; the estimated length of commitment and triple it. From that we can begin to understand the scope and importance of the decision we are making to intervene. Only by understanding the problem and potential costs can we make a coherent appraisal of whether America should intervene.

Overarching Principles

Any appraisal of intervention must begin with two principles that should govern our willingness to intervene for humanitarian reasons.

First, we must respect the absolute requirement to husband the power and freedom of action needed to protect our own strategic interests. To do otherwise is to dissipate our capacity to serve others no less than ourselves. The cost of losing or significantly degrading the power of the United States is a price the world can ill afford.

Second, we must recognize that power in and of itself is amoral. Applied recklessly or with too little forethought, it enables the powerful to do harm as well as good. We possess unequaled potential to cause death, damage, and unintended evil. We are the founding member of an exclusive club that can destroy civilization within minutes. Our actions, particularly interventions, can upset regions, nations, cultures, economies, and peoples, however virtuous our purpose. We must ensure that the cure we offer through intervention is not worse than the disease. In the passion of crisis action planning, these principles must remain central to any option or action we consider.

Criteria for Evaluation

No crisis is a clean mathematical equation against which we can apply perfect and precise metrics. The number of innocent people killed, homes destroyed, or refugees displaced are not variables producing a sum that resolves the case for or against intervention. Most crises are confused and dirty situations, offering only an array of negative and painful choices. Even afterwards their solutions are elusive and the subject of endless controversy. Nothing can relieve us of the responsibility for judgment in every instance.

While we cannot fool ourselves into trying to overstructure or quantify our decision-making process, we can give it rigor. Applying five key criteria provides a useful tool for our evaluation of any prospective intervention: our goals should be to maintain our legitimacy, legality, morality, credibility, and capability.

1.) Legitimacy

Legitimacy is a two-edged sword that cuts across both intervention and a failure to intervene. Our actions, or inaction, and our very leadership, must be accepted in the eyes of the world community. Legitimacy is a prerequisite for any hope of long-term success in an intervention and must be based on a scrupulous assessment of the situation. We must remember that what to one person can seem to be an absolute imperative to intervene can seem to another to be a gross violation of national sovereignty. What we view as humanitarian intervention to protect the weak, others can view as taking sides and upsetting regional evolution.

Conversely, what we view as reasonable hesitation to intervene can be viewed as timidity, racism, or blatant self-interest. As the preeminent power, our legitimacy suffers by our failure to act when the cause is just and the need apparent. If our leadership is to endure, we must be viewed as rational, fair, humane, and consistent.

It is important to our legitimacy to remember that humanitarian crises are not America's responsibility alone; they are a summons to action by the world community. As a primary rule of policy, the United States must give preference to international, rather than unilateral, response to such crises.

A solid first step in both testing and building legitimacy for an intervention is our ability to gain the support of the United Nations and to gather other nations to the cause. Their contributions do not have to be on parity with those we bring, but their willingness to commit, to add their national prestige to the cause, and to accept risks does much to ensure the legitimacy of the operation. Our operations and presence in Korea from 1950 to the present have brought tremendous stability to the region and benefited immeasurably from being an international commitment. That said, when necessary we can go it alone, but the need to act in isolation should give us serious pause.

Another way to protect our legitimacy is to subject the proposed intervention to several commonsense questions:

- Is the wrong or injustice we confront so grave that it warrants outside intervention?

- Is the pressure to act simply a reflection of our own impatience with the speed of the political or social development of a nation or region?

- Have we considered the unintended consequences that accompany every intervention?

- Would U.S. intervention damage relationships and organizations, such as the United Nations, that have become essential to civilized relations among nations?

Filtering our own proposed actions through a hardheaded analysis of this kind will do much to ensure that they will stand the inevitable scrutiny of world opinion.

2.) Legality
Like legitimacy, the legality of our actions is critical. Without a persuasive legal basis, our interventions can be considered invasions. Military power is not self-justifying; it does not automat-

ically provide its own legal basis for action. America has always rejected the realpolitik idea that might makes right.

We must weigh the legal ramifications of every contemplated intervention. Any violation we may commit, however well intentioned, risks condemnation that will sap our moral authority. Calls for holding NATO military personnel individually responsible for allegedly criminal consequences of combat in Kosovo in 1999 is a sobering reminder that as international law is strengthened, it limits all the actors, not just our foes.

Furthermore, pop culture slogans notwithstanding, globalization has not produced a borderless planet. The concept of sovereignty, carefully developed since the rise of the nation-state, remains the very foundation of world order, and it is in our interest to respect it. We must recognize that the more tenuous a nation's hold on its sovereignty, the more jealously it guards it. Concern for the individual rights of a nation's citizenry must be balanced with a sensitivity to the sovereignty of the state. Nations do not evolve in perfect parade-ground step with one another. We do well to recall that scarcely 140 years ago our own nation's practice of slavery was seriously offensive to much of the world. Yet we would have felt violated had other states intervened to right that wrong before we finally did.

That is not to say that we can condone those nations or leaders guilty of violating human rights—far from it. But our crusade for justice must be a mature one. Calibrated pressures and diplomatic leverage are often more effective in the long run than overt military intervention. Briefly, as we demand compliance with international law by others, and may even use our power to enforce it, we must also be willing to abide by law.

3.) Morality

A sure sense of moral conduct must underpin our every action. Much of our hard-won legitimacy as a world leader is built on a general respect for America's moral purpose. No doubt our moral ambition exceeds our achievement, at home no less than abroad. Yet, even falling short as individuals and nations always do, America shines as a beacon of moral example in a world too often darkened by ignoble aims.

Morality is, and must remain, our compass. Surrender it to expediency and our place in the world is doomed. Rational national interests are perfectly accepted motivations for many actions, but we must ensure that those actions are not viewed as immoral, either in motive or execution. The motivation for intervention must be genuinely and obviously humanitarian. History is replete with conquests thinly veiled as interventions to protect a minority population, and the world remembers. In our own case, expedience in the interest of Cold War power struggles or in pursuit of business interests produced actions and repercussions that have haunted our relations with some countries for decades. Accounts of CIA-supported coups in Guatemala and Iran, dealings with unsavory characters in Southeast Asia, and support for anticommunist dictators in several countries have cost us far more than any short-term advantage they might have produced.

As we consider intervention we should pose a broad question that spans both our motivation and the likely outcome: Can we be confident of doing more good than harm, both in the immediate situation and in the wider effort to shape a global regime of stability and restraint in the use of force?

Just as intervention must be moral in motivation, so must it be in execution. The end does not justify the means. Interventions to prevent or eliminate murder or gross injustice cannot sanction that same conduct by our own forces or allies—or by those we seek to assist.

This goes to the individual level. Whenever we contemplate sending young men and women into operations, we must ensure that what we have asked them to do does not put them in unavoidable moral minefields. We must resist the temptation to have "dirty work" done on the side for what we've told them are higher moral purposes. As a philosopher once said, "To do evil that good may result is for bunglers in politics, no less than in morals."

4.) Credibility

Our credibility is precious. Other nations must believe not only in our intentions but in our ability and commitment to deliver on those intentions. We must actually accomplish what we say we will do. Before we commit the nation, we must realistically appraise our ability to deliver on our promises.

We must first be credible to ourselves. Commitments to action by the United States must carry the support of the American people and their elected representatives in Congress. The sometimes painful process a president must endure to gather support for intervention is an essential step in consideration of sometimes costly and often prolonged commitments. Failure to gather support for the long term can cause serious problems as the costs rise.

We see that now. More than a year after the United States led the NATO bombing campaign that began our involvement in Kosovo, the administration is being forced to respond to calls for rapid disengagement. Many members of the House and Senate have voted that all further funding for U.S. operations in Kosovo be tied to a plan for establishing an all-European peacekeeping force or for an early deadline to withdraw American troops.

With almost 4,000 American soldiers still in Bosnia over four years after the Dayton agreement, and a functioning, multi-ethnic Bosnia-Herzegovina a generation or more away, it is not surprising that Americans are seeking to limit yet another occupation.

After following U.S. leadership into bombing Serbia over the issue of Kosovo, and facing increasing violence between Serbs and Albanians in the battered province, it is little wonder that Europeans question the commitment, and ultimately the credibility, of an America seemingly reluctant to help finish what it has started.

So we must be honest to ourselves and to our allies about what we can and will do. Disingenuous promises or half-hearted efforts can vastly increase the suffering we sought to reduce. Our record over the decades is far from blameless. The pointless loss of life among the poorly prepared and weakly supported Cuban exiles at the Bay of Pigs, the brutal subjugation of Kurds in Iraq in 1991, the bloodshed by Hungarian freedom fighters calling for our help in 1956—these tragic episodes demonstrated the cost of hollow promises, however indirect or implied. We must not raise false hopes.

Good intentions are not enough. We must be able to achieve what we attempt to do. Like toothless gestures, failed operations can make situations much worse. Our decade-long debacle in Vietnam carried costs to our power and prestige that were difficult to recoup. So did a single night at Desert One in Iran in 1980. Any apparent or perceived impotence on America's part may embolden others to take steps that greatly increase both the short-term and the long-term damage. A scholar once said that "prestige is to power as credit is to cash." We dare not squander American prestige in feckless adventures.

5.) Capability

Finally, retaining our capability to act effectively in the larger arena is more important than any single crisis or event clamoring for our intervention, for our strength is finite and its loss unacceptable. Every intervention saps resources, expends military power, and taps domestic political will.

Every day of the year we have thousands of American soldiers, sailors, airmen, and marines deployed in humanitarian and peacekeeping missions around the world. They are patrolling the hills of Bosnia and the skies of Iraq, manning guard posts in Kosovo, running support bases in Hungary and Albania, serving as multinational observers in the Sinai, and conducting a host of other tasks we have given them. They are great young people, professional and committed to their missions. Many are part-time soldiers, away from family and jobs, often at significant personal sacrifice.

Their service is magnificent, yet it often masks a larger cost, because what they are doing in these humanitarian deployments, while important, is secondary to their primary purpose of defending America and her vital interests. Anything we do that distracts them from preparing for that essential task must be carefully weighed against the potential consequences.

On a national level, an army that is 40 percent smaller than the force of 784,000 that fought and supported Operation Desert Storm in 1991 had an average of 27,000 soldiers deployed every day of 1999. Another 123,000 are forward-based in places like Korea and Europe. That math tells a serious story. Leaders and soldiers at every level are stretched thin to maintain a force capable of meeting the needs of the nation.

On an individual level the data is more anecdotal, but equally powerful. Challenges with recruiting and retention, extended family separations for a force that is now largely married, and an increased reliance on already strained reserve components mean that each new commitment carries serious costs.

The military's primary mission is fighting and winning major theater wars. Recent humanitarian operations have taxed the military's operating and personnel tempo, causing readiness to slip in some units. Spare parts shortfalls, undermanned units, and recruitment and retention challenges illustrate the phenomenon. The military is simply not organized, trained, equipped, or funded at present to respond adequately to this range and number of humanitarian interventions. If you continue or amplify this willingness to deploy force for such operations, certain changes in the military's orientation must be made.

On a macro level, it may require accepting ever higher risk in our ability to execute the national military strategy of fighting two major theater wars, revising that strategy to be less ambitious, or substantially increasing the defense budget. On a planning level, such humanitarian interventionism would require the development of novel organizational structures more suitable to these kinds of missions, the adaptation of the armed services' training and doctrine regimens (which may come at the expense of other warfighting skills), and the equipping of our men and women in uniform with new and added technological capabilities. These changes are significant. We would need a protracted and extensive discussion within the executive branch (involving military and civilian officials) and even more so with Congress before going down this road.

Like any other resource, political will and domestic support are finite and must be husbanded. Despite the courage and heroic sacrifices of our troops, the United States limped out of Vietnam a greatly weakened power. We withdrew from Lebanon a less credible factor in that nation's civil strife. We came home from Somalia disillusioned by the dreadful sight of American bodies dragged through the streets—and by a sense of futility in a humanitarian effort. If the Gulf War stands as vindication of our nation's determination to resist aggression, these dramatic failures remind us that our power and will are not unlimited. We must comprehend and calculate the costs of each action.

THE BALANCED RESULT

So where would the policy outlined in this memorandum actually lead us? If we accept our role as the world's most powerful nation and balance our strategic interests with a clear responsibility to be a positive and moral force in the world, the result will be neither rash interventionism nor splendid isolation.

Where clear strategic interests such as vital resources or waterways, or overwhelming moral imperatives such as genocide are identified, there would be a powerful rationale for intervention. Even in these cases, however, action would depend on an assessment of what lies within our capability, what it will cost in lives and treasure, and whether we can build domestic support and gather international participation for action. In clear cases, this need not be time-consuming, but it is essential to get it right.

Placed against this model it is unlikely we would have intervened in Lebanon in 1982. No clear strategic interests drove intervention there and positive results were not attainable within the level of commitment we were willing to make.

Rwanda in 1994 would have been compelling. Although no strategic interests were present, the incredible butchery for largely ethnic reasons warranted any effort that would help. Arguments that the remote location precluded effective intervention are unconvincing. Saving a portion of the more than 500,000 souls reportedly murdered, and showing the world that we will never stand idly by while genocide proceeds, would have justified the cost.

Kosovo in 1999 would have been a difficult case. Reports of ethnic cleansing were alarming and Slobodan Milosevic has been a vexing and evil force in the region, but the actions of the somewhat suspect KLA and the lack of a clearly thought-out end state result should have caused further reflection. As events have unfolded thus far, it also appears that a number of nations failed either to understand or to accept the long-term costs of intervention. Whatever the outcome might have been, we failed to think this through adequately before we began to bomb.

Regardless of our personal feelings or emotions, we cannot recommend a policy of open-ended commitment to accept humanitarian claims on our conscience and resources. The right policy for America is one of careful, discriminating balance. A truly humane policy must rest on a rational calculation and a measured process that can guide us through emotional, often media-hyped debates on intervention. Such calculation is not cold-hearted; it is clear-headed. Only a judicious synthesis of our moral values and our strategic interests can define a policy that is sustainable in future humanitarian interventions. The essential fairness and prudence that underlie such a policy are indispensable to building support at home and abroad for those humanitarian operations we choose to undertake.

The awesome responsibility that has come to bear on the United States dictates that we exercise utmost maturity and caution in the use of our power. We must do what we can, but protect what we can do. We must be a force for good in the world, a last-resort defense for the defenseless. But when all is said and done we must conserve that power to do good—both for the protection of the nation, and for our long-term service to the world.

BACKGROUND MATERIALS

APPENDIX A

THE CLINTON DOCTRINE

In the immediate aftermath of the Kosovo war, President William Clinton indicated that the conflict established a new precedent for future U.S. response to similar crises. The president's remarks described what became known as the "Clinton Doctrine" on humanitarian intervention.

THE WHITE HOUSE

Office of the Press Secretary
(Skopje, Macedonia)

For Immediate Release   June 22, 1999

REMARKS BY THE PRESIDENT
TO THE KFOR TROOPS

Skopje, Macedonia Airport
Skopje, Macedonia

5:43 P.M. (L)

THE PRESIDENT: Thank you very much, General Clark, General Jackson, General Craddock, Colonel Ingram; ladies and gentlemen of the United States military. And as nearly as I can tell, we've got a few of our British counterparts back there, and at least two Spanish officers over here somewhere.

And I just want to say, first of all, I am proud to have the soldiers, the Marines, the airmen and women, the Naval forces of the United States of America serving in NATO. I am proud that we're part of KFOR. I'm proud that we're serving under an able commander like General Jackson. I am proud of Wes Clark.

You know, General Clark and I went through the agony of Bosnia together. He lost three good friends, who fell off a mountain because Mr. Milosevic wouldn't let them take the safe road to try to negotiate a peace. And we watched for four years while reasoned diplomacy tried to save lives, and a quarter of a million people died and two and a half million refugees were created before NATO and our friends on the ground in Croatia and Bosnia forced a settlement there and ended the horror there.

This time, we didn't wait. And it took 79 days, but that's a lot better than four years. And I hope the people of the world, when they see these horrible, horrible stories coming out, the mass graves and all of that, just imagine what it would have been like if we had stepped to the side and not done what we did for the last three months.

I hope to the day you die, you will be proud of being a part of the nation and a democratic alliance that believes that people should not be killed, uprooted or destroyed because of their race, their ethnic background or the way they worship God. I am proud of that, and I hope you are.

Let me also say to you that I just came from one of our refugee camps, and there are a lot of grateful people there. But you and I know that there's a lot to be done yet, and General Jackson's got a big job. And the United States is proud to be doing our part to help our allied efforts succeed there. We must not have one conflict and roll back ethnic cleansing and then lose the peace because we don't do every last thing just as we're supposed to do it.

So the whole credibility of the principle on which we have stood our ground and fought in this region for years and years now— that here, just like in America, just like in Great Britain, people who come from different racial and ethnic and religious backgrounds can live together and work together and do better together if they simply respect each other's God-given dignity—and we don't want our children to grow up in a 21st century world where innocent civilians can be hauled off to the slaughter, where children can die en masse, where young boys of military age can be burned alive, where young girls can be raped en masse just to intimidate their families—we don't want our kids to grow up in a world like that.

Now, what it rides on is not the precision of our bombs, not in our power to destroy, but your power to build—and to be safe while you're doing it and to protect the ethnic Kosovar Albanians and the ethnic Serbs alike. As long as they are innocent civilians, doing nothing wrong, they're entitled to protection. And to try to show by the power of your example, day in and day out, those of you that are going into Kosovo, that people can lay down their hatreds.

You need to think about telling your family stories. You need to think about how we can help these people get over this awful, grievous thing. I saw a lot of little kids just a few minutes ago with a lot of hurt and terror and loss in their eyes. So you've got a big, big job left.

It is not free of danger, it will not be free of difficulty. There will be some days you wish you were somewhere else. But never forget if we can do this here, and if we can then say to the people of the world, whether you live in Africa, or Central Europe, or any other place, if somebody comes after innocent civilians and tries to kill them en masse because of their race, their ethnic background or their religion, and it's within our power to stop it, we will stop it.

And, by the way, look at Central Europe. These people can live together and prosper together. That's what we're trying to do. It can make a huge difference to our children in the new century. It may mean that Americans will never have to fight again in a big land war, because we just let things get out of hand and out of hand and out of hand until everything blew up and there was nothing else that could be done about it. This is very important.

And, again, I say I hope you will always be proud of it. I hope you know how proud that I and the American people are of you. Thank you and God bless you.

APPENDIX B

PRESIDENTIAL DECISION DIRECTIVE 56 ON "COMPLEX CONTINGENCY OPERATIONS"

U.S. planning for various humanitarian contingencies has been guided by a Presidential Decision Directive (PDD 56) issued in May 1997. The essential features of that directive are described in an unclassified "white paper."

PURPOSE

This White Paper explains key elements of the Clinton Administration's policy on managing complex contingency operations. This unclassified document is promulgated for use by government officials as a handy reference for interagency planning of future complex contingency operations. Also, it is intended for use in U.S. Government professional education institutions, such as the National Defense University and the National Foreign Affairs Training Center, for coursework and exercises on interagency practices and procedures. Regarding this paper's utility as representation of the President's Directive, it contains all the key elements of the original PDD that are needed for effective implementation by agency officials. Therefore, wide dissemination of this unclassified White Paper is encouraged by all agencies of the U.S. Government. Note that while this White Paper explains the PDD, it does not override the official PDD.

BACKGROUND

In the wake of the Cold War, attention has focused on a rising number of territorial disputes, armed ethnic conflicts, and civil wars that pose threats to regional and international peace and may be accompanied by natural or manmade disasters which precipitate massive human suffering. We have learned that effective responses to these situations may require multi-dimensional operations composed of such components as political/diplomatic, humanitarian, intelligence, economic development, and security: hence the term complex contingency operations.

The PDD defines "complex contingency operations" as peace operations such as the peace accord implementation operation conducted by NATO in Bosnia (1995–present) and the humanitarian intervention in northern Iraq called Operation Provide Comfort (1991); and foreign humanitarian assistance operations, such as Operation Support Hope in central Africa (1994) and Operation Sea Angel in Bangladesh (1991). Unless otherwise directed, this PDD does not apply to domestic disaster relief or to relatively routine or small-scale operations, nor to military operations conducted in defense of U.S. citizens, territory, or property, including counter-terrorism and hostage-rescue operations and international armed conflict.

In recent situations as diverse as Haiti, Somalia, Northern Iraq, and the former Yugoslavia, the United States has engaged in complex contingency operations in coalition, either under the auspices of an international or regional organization or in ad hoc, temporary coalitions of like-minded states. While never relinquishing the capability to respond unilaterally, the PDD assumes that the U.S. will continue to conduct future operations in coalition whenever possible.

We must also be prepared to manage the humanitarian, economic and political consequences of a technological crisis where chemical, biological, and/or radiological hazards may be present. The occurrence of any one of these dimensions could significantly increase the sensitivity and complexity of a U.S. response to a technological crisis.

In many complex emergencies the appropriate U.S. Government response will incur the involvement of only non-military assets.

In some situations, we have learned that military forces can quickly affect the dynamics of the situation and may create the conditions necessary to make significant progress in mitigating or resolving underlying conflict or dispute. However, we have also learned that many aspects of complex emergencies may not be best addressed through military measures. Furthermore, given the level of U.S. interests at stake in most of these situations, we recognize that U.S. forces should not be deployed in an operation indefinitely.

It is essential that the necessary resources be provided to ensure that we are prepared to respond in a robust, effective manner. To foster a durable peace or stability in these situations and to maximize the effect of judicious military deployments, the civilian components of an operation must be integrated closely with the military components.

While agencies of government have developed independent capacities to respond to complex emergencies, military and civilian agencies should operate in a synchronized manner through effective interagency management and the use of special mechanisms to coordinate agency efforts. Integrated planning and effective management of agency operations early on in an operation can avoid delays, reduce pressure on the military to expand its involvement in unplanned ways, and create unity of effort within an operation that is essential for success of the mission.

INTENT OF THE PDD

The need for complex contingency operations is likely to recur in future years, demanding varying degrees of U.S. involvement. The PDD calls for all U.S. Government agencies to institutionalize what we have learned from our recent experiences and to continue the process of improving the planning and management of complex contingency operations. The PDD is designed to ensure that the lessons learned—including proven planning processes and implementation mechanisms—will be incorporated into the interagency process on a regular basis.

The PDD's intent is to establish these management practices to achieve unity of effort among U.S. Government agencies and international organizations engaged in complex contingency operations. Dedicated mechanisms and integrated planning processes are needed. From our recent experiences, we have learned that these can help to: identify appropriate missions and tasks, if any, for U.S. Government agencies in a U.S. Government response; develop strategies for early resolution of crises, thereby minimizing the loss of life and establishing the basis for reconciliation and reconstruction; accelerate planning and implementation of the civilian aspects of the operation; intensify action on critical funding and personnel requirements early on; integrate all components of a U.S. response (civilian, military, police, etc.) at the policy level and facilitate the creation of coordination mechanisms at the operational level; and rapidly identify issues for senior policy makers and ensure expeditious implementation of decisions.

The PDD requires all agencies to review their legislative and budget authorities for supporting complex contingency operations and, where such authorities are inadequate to fund an agency's mission and operations in complex contingencies, propose legislative and budgetary solutions.

EXECUTIVE COMMITTEE

The PDD calls upon the Deputies Committee to establish appropriate interagency working groups to assist in policy development, planning, and execution of complex contingency operations. Normally, the Deputies Committee will form an Executive Committee (ExCom) with appropriate membership to supervise the day-to-day management of U.S. participation in a complex contingency operation. The ExCom will bring together representatives of all agencies that might participate in the operation, including those not normally part of the NSC structure. When this is the case, both the Deputies Committee and the ExCom will normally be augmented by participating agency representatives. In addition, the chair of the ExCom will normally designate an agency to lead a legal and fiscal advisory sub-group, whose role is to consult with the ExCom to ensure that tasks assigned by the ExCom can be performed by the assigned agencies consistent with legal and fiscal authorities. This ExCom approach has proved useful in clarifying agency responsibilities, strengthening agency accountability, ensuring interagency coordination, and developing policy options for consideration by senior policy makers.

The guiding principle behind the ExCom approach to interagency management is the personal accountability of presidential appointees. Members of the ExCom effectively serve as functional managers for specific elements of the U.S. Government response (e.g., refugees, demobilization, elections, economic assistance, police reform, public information, etc.). They implement the strategies agreed to by senior policy makers in the interagency and report to the ExCom and Deputies Committee on any problems or issues that need to be resolved.

In future complex contingency operations to which the United States contributes substantial resources, the PDD calls upon the Deputies Committee to establish organizational arrangements akin to those of the ExCom approach.

THE POLITICAL-MILITARY IMPLEMENTATION PLAN

The PDD requires that a political-military implementation plan (or "pol-mil plan") be developed as an integrated planning tool for coordinating U.S. government actions in a complex contingency operation. The pol-mil plan will include a comprehensive situation assessment, mission statement, agency objectives, and desired end state. It will outline an integrated concept of operations to synchronize agency efforts. The plan will identify the primary preparatory issues and tasks for conducting an operation (e.g., congressional consultations, diplomatic efforts, troop recruitment, legal authorities, funding requirements and sources, media coordination, etc.). It will also address major functional mission area tasks (e.g., political mediation/reconciliation, military support, demobilization, humanitarian assistance, police reform, basic public services, economic restoration, human rights monitoring, social reconciliation, public information, etc.). (Annex A contains an illustrative outline of a pol-mil plan.)

With the use of the pol-mil plan, the interagency can implement effective management practices, namely, to centralize planning and decentralize execution during the operation. The desired unity of effort among the various agencies that is created through the use of the pol-mil plan contributes to the overall success of these complex operations.

When a complex contingency operation is contemplated in which the U.S. Government will play a substantial role, the PDD calls upon the Deputies Committee to task the development of a pol-mil plan and assign specific responsibilities to the appropriate ExCom officials.

Each ExCom official will be required to develop their respective part of the plan, which will be fully coordinated among all relevant agencies. This development process will be transparent and analytical, resulting in issues being posed to senior policy makers for resolution. Based on the resulting decisions, the plan will be finalized and widely distributed among relevant agencies.

The PDD also requires that the pol-mil plan include demonstrable milestones and measures of success including detailed planning for the transition of the operation to activities which might be performed by a follow-on operation or by the host government. According to the PDD, the pol-mil plan should be updated as the mission progresses to reflect milestones that are (or are not) met and to incorporate changes in the situation on the ground.

INTERAGENCY POL-MIL PLAN REHEARSAL

A critical aspect of the planning process will be the interagency rehearsal/review of the pol-mil plan. As outlined in the PDD, this activity involves a rehearsal of the plan's main elements, with the appropriate ExCom official presenting the elements for which he or she is responsible. By simultaneously rehearsing/reviewing all elements of the plan, differences over mission objectives, agency responsibilities, timing/synchronization, and resource allocation can be identified and resolved early, preferably before the operation begins. The interagency rehearsal/review also underscores the accountability of each program manager in implementing their assigned area of responsibility. During execution, regular reviews of the plan ensure that milestones are met and that appropriate adjustments are made.

The PDD calls upon the Deputies Committee to conduct the interagency rehearsal/review of the pol-mil plan. Supporting agency plans are to be presented by ExCom officials before a complex contingency operation is launched (or as early as possible once the operation begins), before a subsequent critical phase during the operation, as major changes in the mission occur, and prior to an operation's termination.

AFTER-ACTION REVIEW

After the conclusion of each operation in which this planning process is employed, the PDD directs the ExCom to charter an after-action review involving both those who participated in the operation and Government experts who monitored its execution. This comprehensive assessment of interagency performance will include a review of interagency planning and coordination (both in Washington and in the field), legal and budgetary difficulties encountered, problems in agency execution, as well as proposed solutions, in order to capture lessons learned and to ensure their dissemination to relevant agencies.

TRAINING

The U.S. Government requires the capacity to prepare agency officials for the responsibilities they will be expected to take on in planning and managing agency efforts in a complex contingency operation. Creating a cadre of professionals familiar with this integrated planning process will improve the USG's [U.S. Government's] ability to manage future operations.

In the interest of advancing the expertise of government officials, agencies are encouraged to disseminate the Handbook for Interagency Management of Complex Contingency Operations published by OASD (S&R) at (703) 614-0421.

With the support of the State and Defense Departments, the PDD requires the NSC to work with the appropriate U.S. Government educational institutions—including the National Defense University, the National Foreign Affairs Training Center and the Army War College—to develop and conduct an interagency training program. This program, which should be held at least annually, will train mid-level managers (Deputy Assistant Secretary level) in the development and implementation of pol-mil plans for complex contingency operations. Those participating should have an opportunity to interact with expert officials from previous operations to learn what has worked in the past. Also, the PDD calls upon appropriate U.S. government educational institutions to explore the appropriate way to incorporate the pol-mil planning process into their curricula.

AGENCY REVIEW AND IMPLEMENTATION

Finally, the PDD directs each agency to review the adequacy of their agency's structure, legal authorities, budget levels, personnel system, training, and crisis management procedures to insure that we, as a government, are learning from our experiences with complex contingency operations and institutionalizing the lessons learned.

ANNEX A: ILLUSTRATIVE COMPONENTS OF A POLITICAL-MILITARY PLAN FOR A COMPLEX CONTINGENCY OPERATION

Situation Assessment. A comprehensive assessment of the situation to clarify essential information that, in the aggregate, provides a multi-dimensional picture of the crisis.

U.S. Interests. A statement of U.S. interests at stake in the crisis and the requirement to secure those interests.

Mission Statement. A clear statement of the USG's strategic purpose for the operation and the pol-mil mission.

Objectives. The key civil-military objectives to be accomplished during the operation.

Desired Pol-Mil End State. The conditions the operation is intended to create before the operation transitions to a follow-on operation and/or terminates.

Concept of the Operation. A conceptual description of how the various instruments of USG policy will be integrated to get the job done throughout all phases of the operation.

Lead Agency Responsibilities. An assignment of responsibilities for participating agencies.

Transition/Exit Strategy. A strategy that is linked to the realization of the end state described above, requiring the integrated efforts of diplomats, military leaders, and relief officials of the USG and the international community.

Organizational Concept. A schematic of the various organizational structures of the operation, in Washington and in theater, including a description of the chain of authority and associated reporting channels.

Preparatory Tasks. A layout of specific tasks to be undertaken before the operation begins (congressional consultations, diplomatic efforts, troop recruitment, legal authorities, funding requirements and sources, media coordination, etc.).

Functional or Mission Area Tasks/Agency Plans. Key operational and support plans written by USG agencies that pertain to critical parts of the operation (e.g., political mediation/reconciliation, military support, demobilization, humanitarian assistance, police reform, basic public services, economic restoration, human rights monitoring, social reconciliation, public information, etc.).

APPENDIX C

THE U.N. SECRETARY-GENERAL ON HUMANITARIAN INTERVENTION

On September 20, 1999 U.N. Secretary-General Kofi Annan reviewed the tension between the traditional legal concept of the sovereign state, immune to outside interference in its internal affairs, and the emerging pressures for international intervention to curb humanitarian abuses. Following are excerpts from his address to the U.N. General Assembly.

... [O]n this occasion, I shall like to address the prospects for human security and intervention in the next century. In light of the dramatic events of the past year, I trust that you will understand this decision.

As Secretary-General, I have made it my highest duty to restore the United Nations to its rightful role in the pursuit of peace and security, and to bring it closer to the peoples it serves. As we stand at the brink of a new century, this mission continues.

But it continues in a world transformed by geo-political, economic, technological and environmental changes whose lasting significance still eludes us. As we seek new ways to combat the ancient enemies of war and poverty, we will succeed only if we all adapt our Organization to a world with new actors, new responsibilities, and new possibilities for peace and progress.

State sovereignty, in its most basic sense, is being redefined by the forces of globalization and international cooperation.

The State is now widely understood to be the servant of its people, and not vice versa. At the same time, individual sovereignty—and by this I mean the human rights and fundamental freedoms of each and every individual as enshrined in our Charter—has been enhanced by a renewed consciousness of the right of every individual to control his or her own destiny.

These parallel developments—remarkable and, in many ways, welcome—do not lend themselves to easy interpretations or simple conclusions.

They do, however, demand of us a willingness to think anew —about how the United Nations responds to the political, human rights and humanitarian crises affecting so much of the world; about the means employed by the international community in situations of need; and about our willingness to act in some areas of conflict, while limiting ourselves to humanitarian palliatives in many other crises whose daily toll of death and suffering ought to shame us into action.

Our reflections on these critical questions derive not only from the events of last year, but from a variety of challenges that confront us today, most urgently in East Timor.

From Sierra Leone to the Sudan to Angola to the Balkans to Cambodia and to Afghanistan, there are a great number of peoples who need more than just words of sympathy from the international community. They need a real and sustained commitment to help end their cycles of violence, and launch them on a safe passage to prosperity.

While the genocide in Rwanda will define for our generation the consequences of inaction in the face of mass murder, the more recent conflict in Kosovo has prompted important questions about the consequences of action in the absence of complete unity on the part of the international community.

It has cast in stark relief the dilemma of what has been called humanitarian intervention: on one side, the question of the legitimacy of an action taken by a regional organization without a United Nations mandate; on the other, the universally recognized imperative of effectively halting gross and systematic violations of human rights with grave humanitarian consequences.

The inability of the international community in the case of Kosovo to reconcile these two equally compelling interests—universal legitimacy and effectiveness in defence of human rights—can only be viewed as a tragedy.

It has revealed the core challenge to the Security Council and to the United Nations as a whole in the next century: to forge unity behind the principle that massive and systematic violations of human rights—wherever they may take place—should not be allowed to stand.

The Kosovo conflict and its outcome have prompted a wide debate of profound importance to the resolution of conflicts from the Balkans to Central Africa to East Asia. And to each side in this critical debate, difficult questions can be posed.

To those for whom the greatest threat to the future of international order is the use of force in the absence of a Security Council mandate, one might ask—not in the context of Kosovo—but in the context of Rwanda: If, in those dark days and hours leading up to the genocide, a coalition of States had been prepared to act in defence of the Tutsi population, but did not receive prompt Council authorization, should such a coalition have stood aside and allowed the horror to unfold?

To those for whom the Kosovo action heralded a new era when States and groups of States can take military action outside the established mechanisms for enforcing international law, one might ask: Is there not a danger of such interventions undermining the imperfect, yet resilient, security system created after the Second World War, and of setting dangerous precedents for future interventions without a clear criterion to decide who might invoke these precedents, and in what circumstances?

... In response to this turbulent era of crises and interventions, there are those who have suggested that the Charter itself—with its roots in the aftermath of global inter-State war—is ill-suited to guide us in a world of ethnic wars and intra-State violence. I believe they are wrong.

The Charter is a living document, whose high principles still define the aspirations of peoples everywhere for lives of peace, dignity and development. Nothing in the Charter precludes a recognition that there are rights beyond borders.

Indeed, its very letter and spirit are the affirmation of those fundamental human rights. In short, it is not the deficiencies of the Charter which have brought us to this juncture, but our difficulties in applying its principles to a new era; an era when strictly traditional notions of sovereignty can no longer do justice to the aspirations of peoples everywhere to attain their fundamental freedoms.

The sovereign States who drafted the Charter over half a century ago were dedicated to peace, but experienced in war.

They knew the terror of conflict, but knew equally that there are times when the use of force may be legitimate in the pursuit of peace. That is why the Charter's own words declare that "armed force shall not be used, save in the common interest." But what is that common interest? Who shall define it? Who will defend it? Under whose authority? And with what means of intervention? These are the monumental questions facing us as we enter the new century. While I will not propose specific answers or criteria, I shall identify four aspects of intervention which I believe hold important lessons for resolving future conflicts.

First, it is important to define intervention as broadly as possible, to include actions along a wide continuum from the most pacific to the most coercive. A tragic irony of many of the crises that continue to go unnoticed and unchallenged today is that they could be dealt with by far less perilous acts of intervention than the one we witnessed recently in Yugoslavia. And yet, the commitment of the international community to peacekeeping, to humanitarian assistance, to rehabilitation and reconstruction varies greatly from region to region, and crisis to crisis.

If the new commitment to intervention in the face of extreme suffering is to retain the support of the world's peoples, it must be—and must be seen to be—fairly and consistently applied, irrespective of region or nation. Humanity, after all, is indivisible.

It is also necessary to recognize that any armed intervention is itself a result of the failure of prevention. As we consider the future of intervention, we must redouble our efforts to enhance our preventive capabilities—including early warning, preventive diplomacy, preventive deployment and preventive disarmament.

A recent powerful tool of deterrence has been the actions of the Tribunals for Rwanda and the former Yugoslavia. In their battle against impunity lies a key to deterring crimes against humanity. Even the costliest policy of prevention is far cheaper, in lives and in resources, than the least expensive use of armed force.

Second, it is clear that sovereignty alone is not the only obstacle to effective action in human rights or humanitarian crises. No less significant are the ways in which the Member States of the United Nations define their national interest in any given crisis.

Of course, the traditional pursuit of national interest is a permanent feature of international relations and of the life and work of the Security Council. But as the world has changed in profound ways since the end of the Cold War, I believe our conceptions of national interest have failed to follow suit.

A new, more broadly defined, more widely conceived definition of national interest in the new century would, I am convinced, induce States to find far greater unity in the pursuit of such basic Charter values as democracy, pluralism, human rights, and the rule of law. A global era requires global engagement. Indeed, in a growing number of challenges facing humanity, the collective interest is the national interest.

Third, in the event that forceful intervention becomes necessary, we must ensure that the Security Council, the body charged with authorizing force under international law, is able to rise to the challenge.

The choice, as I said during the Kosovo conflict, must not be between Council unity and inaction in the face of genocide—as in the case of Rwanda, on the one hand; and Council division, and regional action, as in the case of Kosovo, on the other.

In both cases, the Member States of the United Nations should have been able to find common ground in upholding the principles of the Charter, and acting in defence of our common humanity.

As important as the Council's enforcement power is its deterrent power. Unless it is able to assert itself collectively where the cause is just and where the means are available, its credibility in the eyes of the world may well suffer.

If States bent on criminal behaviour know that frontiers are not the absolute defence; if they know that the Security Council will take action to halt crimes against humanity, then they will not embark on such a course of action in expectation of sovereign impunity.

The Charter requires the Council to be the defender of the common interest, and unless it is seen to be so—in an era of human rights, interdependence, and globalization—there is a danger that others could seek to take its place.

Let me say that the Council's prompt and effective action in authorizing a multinational force for East Timor reflects precisely the unity of purpose that I have called for today. Already, however, far too many lives have been lost and far too much destruction has taken place for us to rest on our laurels. The hard work of bringing peace and stability to East Timor still awaits us.

Finally, after the conflict is over, in East Timor as everywhere, it is vitally important that the commitment to peace be as strong as the commitment to war.

In this situation, too, consistency is essential. Just as our commitment to humanitarian action must be universal if it is to be legitimate, so our commitment to peace cannot end with the cessation of hostilities. The aftermath of war requires no less skill, no less sacrifice, no fewer resources in order to forge a lasting peace and avoid a return to violence.

Kosovo—and other United Nations missions currently deployed or looming over the horizon—presents us with just such a challenge. Unless the United Nations is given the means and support to succeed, not only the peace, but the war, too, will be lost. From civil administration to policing to the creation of a civil society capable of sustaining a tolerant, pluralist, prosperous society, the challenges facing our peacekeeping, peacemaking and peace-building missions are immense.

But if we are given the means—in Kosovo and in Sierra Leone, in East Timor—we have a real opportunity to break the cycles of violence, once and for all.

. . . [J]ust as we have learned that the world cannot stand aside when gross and systematic violations of human rights are taking place, so we have also learned that intervention must be based on legitimate and universal principles if it is to enjoy the sustained support of the world's peoples.

This developing international norm in favour of intervention to protect civilians from wholesale slaughter will no doubt continue to pose profound challenges to the international community.

Any such evolution in our understanding of State sovereignty and individual sovereignty will, in some quarters, be met with distrust, skepticism, even hostility. But it is an evolution that we should welcome.

Why? Because, despite its limitations and imperfections, it is testimony to a humanity that cares more, not less, for the suffering in its midst, and a humanity that will do more, and not less, to end it.

It is a hopeful sign at the end of the twentieth century.

ABOUT THE AUTHORS

HOLLY J. BURKHALTER is the Advocacy Director of Physicians for Human Rights, an organization specializing in medical, scientific and forensic investigations of violations of internationally recognized human rights. She is the Coordinator of the U.S. Campaign to Ban Landmines, part of the international coalition that Physicians for Human Rights helped found and that shared the 1997 Nobel Peace Prize. Ms. Burkhalter served previously as Advocacy Director of Human Rights Watch and as a staff member of the House Foreign Affairs Committee. She testifies frequently before Congress and publishes widely, including a regular column on human rights policy for *Legal Times.*

ALTON FRYE is the Presidential Senior Fellow at the Council on Foreign Relations, where he has also served as President and as National Director. Previously a member of the RAND Corporation and a U.S. Senate staff director, he has taught at UCLA and Harvard. A frequent consultant to Congress and the executive branch, his books include *A Responsible Congress: The Politics of National Security.*

ARNOLD KANTER is a Principal and founding member of the Scowcroft Group, an international business consulting firm. He is also a Senior Fellow at the Forum for International Policy and at the RAND Corporation. From 1991 to 1993 Dr. Kanter was Under Secretary of State, having served in the State Department from 1977 to 1985 and on the staff of the National Security Council from 1989 to 1991. In his private career he has been a program director at RAND and on the Brookings Institution research staff, as well as a faculty member at Ohio State University and the University of Michigan. In addition to service on the Defense Science Board and as an adviser to the intelligence community Dr. Kanter is a director of the Atlantic Council and the Henry L. Stimson Center.

STANLEY A. MCCHRYSTAL is a U.S. Army colonel, currently the Assistant Commander for Operations in the 82nd Airborne Division. During 1999–2000, he was a Military Fellow at the Council on Foreign Relations, where he prepared his contribution to this CPI. A West Point graduate, Colonel McChrystal has been a National Security Fellow at Harvard University's Kennedy School of Government and also holds a master's degree in strategic studies from the Naval War College. He has commanded both airborne and ranger battalions. Among his military honors are the Legion of Merit, the Bronze Star, and the Defense Meritorious Service Medal.

DOV S. ZAKHEIM is Chief Executive Officer of SPC International Corporation and Consultant to the Secretary of Defense. From 1985 until March 1987, Dr. Zakheim was Deputy Under Secretary of Defense for Planning and Resources. He is author of *Flight of the Levi: Inside a U.S.-Israeli Crisis, Congress and National Security in the Post–Cold War Era,* and numerous articles and chapters in books. An Adjunct Senior Fellow of the Council on Foreign Relations, Dr. Zakheim writes, lectures, and provides commentary on national defense and foreign policy issues both domestically and internationally.